Ten Year Plan

How the founders of
Tender Greens scaled
their heart-centered
brand

DAVID DRESSLER
ERIK OBERHOLTZER

Table of Contents

A note from the authors,
David Dressler and Erik Oberholtzer

Tender Greens and the T.Y.P. Restaurant Group, Inc. would not have succeeded without the complementary talents and equal contributions of its three co-founders: David Dressler, Matt Lyman, and Erik Oberholtzer.

Our partnership worked like a tight band of musicians. We were in it together, yet each of us got to solo with support and encouragement from the others. As two of the band members, we felt moved to write this book recounting the unique business all three of us built.

As the authors, it's our blended voices you will be hearing in this book, but every mention of *we, us,* and *our* very much includes and honors our fellow band member, Matt.

Since its inception, Tender Greens was always about a commitment to *we*—*we* the partners, *we* the talented people who became our team members, *we* our suppliers, investors, loyal customers, and neighborhood communities.

While this is very much a book about building a business, in our case it was built one dish at a time. There are so many incredible people who work so hard to create Tender Greens and without whom our business would never have grown.

From time to time, the story will call out a solo performer and refer to Erik, David, Matt or others by name. Our intent is not to confuse but to give credit to individual contributions to what was always a shared success.

Finally, this book would likely not have been written without the thoughtful encouragement of our friend Marilyn Anthony who coaxed, wrangled, and held space for us while we looked back at our successes, failings and thankfully few differing perspectives.

INTRODUCTION

When we—Matt Lyman, David Dressler, and Erik Oberholtzer—formed our company, T.Y.P. Restaurant Group, Inc. and launched our first Tender Greens restaurant, we were well into our 30s. Old enough to have logged significant time in the restaurant industry, but young enough to know we'd still be working for many more years after our Ten Year Plan (T.Y.P.) reached its projected end.

What brought the three of us together was a shared belief that we could build a thriving restaurant business by designing an enterprise model around a set of core values. That belief, plus the need to share our collective courage to stop working for others and stake a claim of our own. We began by creating a company culture that would value all our stakeholders—team members, suppliers, investors, guests, and neighbors.

The business we built, Tender Greens, founded in Los Angeles, California in 2006 is a pioneering "polished casual" brand. Our mission was to make healthy, delicious, locally sourced food available to more than the elite 1% able to afford high-quality restaurants.

In 2014, Conde Nast Traveler named Tender Greens one of "The Ten Best Restaurant Chains in the World." In 2015, Forbes recognized Tender Greens as one of the "25 Most Innovative Consumer Brands."

We designed Tender Greens for growth—not simply to grow profits, but to operate at a volume that would make a difference in the supply chain, provide excellent employment opportunities, offer stable life-supporting careers, and "democratize" healthy, professionally prepared food through economies of scale far greater than we could achieve with a single restaurant.

Our innovative but replicable Ten Year Plan, now one of the cornerstones of David's and Erik's advisory practices for founders and business leaders, enabled Tender Greens to flourish as an innovative business model by:

- Shortening our supply chain to buy direct from growers and producers.
- Making wholesome, locally sourced food more affordable.
- Making suppliers equity partners in our business.
- Investing in our team members and underserved communities.
- Integrating our social mission into our core business and brand identity.
- Creating and fostering a heart-centered culture of holistic human development.

Using our story as illustration, we want to encourage stakeholders at all stages of the supply chain—farmers, growers, producers, buyers, chefs, and consumers to consider the alternative business principles and practices underlying Tender Greens. Our approach shows that a patient, long view applied to business planning, from launch to maturity to eventual liquidity event, works. Even in the fast casual restaurant industry, slow business succeeds. And margins do not have to be sacrificed for mission.

Tender Greens began with us clearly and candidly answering three questions about our new venture:

- Why is this needed?

- Why now?
- Why are we the ones to undertake it?

We believe in the power of "3 Whys" so it seems only fair for us to open this book by explaining what prompted us to write it.

Why is this book needed? We believe that the U.S. economy has drifted into a way of doing business that neglects the main cause of enterprise, which is to *create value,* a different result than mere profit. A purely profit-driven approach does not address the primary reason many "social entrepreneurs" are inspired to start businesses, especially now. People start businesses for many reasons. For us part of the appeal was to create a workplace that gave us the life we wanted and that we believed others craved as well. We wanted to make money and we have no regrets about how we and the people who worked with us earned it. And we wanted the business to contribute to advancing the larger goals of a Triple Bottom Line: people, profit, and planet. We believe that the exclusively profit-driven business model needs to be replaced with a more holistic and human-centric process. Profit helps to fuel and fund the solution but should never be the dominant end goal.

Why now? The Covid-19 pandemic has exposed how deeply flawed and vulnerable our society is in so many ways. Access to healthy food, an essential need for everyone, suddenly seems threatened. As we rebuild our food supply chain, restaurant industry, and our relationship with food, we have the opportunity to make a more just and durable food system. Or we can continue to permit major corporate conglomerates, driven exclusively by profit, to dictate the terms of our food system, with dire consequences for all eaters and the planet.

Why us? Our partnership combines deep experience in both "front and back of the house"—dual views that have given us a holistic perspective on the business of food. Food—its production, distribution, and consumption, can connect us or divide us. It is possibly the greatest engine for social change. The food system is linked to some of our most pressing social issues—environmental degradation through poor agricultural practice, energy consumption through logistics and packaging, pollution and waste, food insecurity, the rise of diet-related illness, and climate change.

Our experience is rooted in the restaurant industry, but our work as advisors and consultants demonstrates that the lessons we learned can benefit founders, owners, and entrepreneurs in a variety of businesses and industries. Regardless of where you are in the life cycle of your business, we hope our story will encourage you to invest in examining your larger goals and the values guiding your day-to-day decisions.

The Tender Greens journey was not a straight, smooth shot. We had hard times, made mistakes, pivoted more than once, and dealt with doubt and uncertainty. But we succeeded by adhering to principles and practices we will share in this book, namely:

- Investing early in a clear statement of values.
- Staying true to those values despite pressures to compromise.
- Being honest and transparent with each other and our stakeholders.
- Working for more than profit.
- Pacing ourselves for the long game.
- Building a community of trusted advisors.
- Learning continuously and humbly.

In year 9 we made good on our goals for Tender Greens T.Y.P. Restaurant Group—one year ahead of schedule, after hitting or surpassing all the benchmarks we had set a decade earlier: revenue, forecasted return on investment for early stage investors, internal company culture, and social impact. For the first time in our lives we achieved substantial financial security. Just as important, we built the Sustainable Life Project, a venture to serve foster youth aging out of care facilities.

This book follows the evolution of our business from idea to start-up, from fledgling to high functioning, through growth to significant scale. In it, we detail the important practices we put in place at Tender Greens and how these helped us achieve our operational, financial, and social impact goals. We explore the stresses, threats, and opportunities present at various stages of growth.

For those in the hospitality industry, we hope you will adopt this approach to help rebuild a more equitable food system. For those in other lines of work, we hope this book encourages you to achieve scale and impact based on your beliefs and values. It may also help you attain a sustainable competitive advantage based on the authenticity of your business operations.

As entrepreneurs, we have been profoundly influenced by the careers of pioneering chefs like Wolfgang Puck and Joachim Splichal who showed the possibilities for scaling high-quality, diverse restaurant operations. Books from a wide range of social entrepreneurs have been even more influential—Whole Foods Market founder John Mackey's "Conscious Capitalism," Clif Bar founder Gary Erickson's "Raising the Bar," Patagonia founder Yvon Chouinard's "Let My People Go Surfing," Union Square Hospitality Group founder Danny Meyer's "Setting the Table," Starbucks CEO Howard Schultz's "Pour Your Heart Into It," and business author Michael Gerber's "The E Myth," to name a few.

Just as we hoped to build a restaurant brand that could stand shoulder to shoulder with Wolfgang's or Joachim's, we hope this book warrants shelf space alongside the works of social impact entrepreneurs we admire. Their frank descriptions of the challenges, dark moments, and breakthroughs they faced as businesspeople have both comforted and inspired us.

We believe the lessons learned building Tender Greens with our Ten Year Plan can be a roadmap and a reassuring resource for readers at any career stage who want their business enterprises and their lives to do and be more. In spite of how it often feels, you are not alone on your journey to create a more equitable, safer, and healthier society through the values-centered businesses you create.

Chapter 1

We Put the Pin in the Map

"Stop wearing your wishbone where your backbone ought to be."
—Elizabeth Gilbert

*W*e wrote this book to take you with us on our journey, the Ten Year Plan that led to Tender Greens' success—our wins, losses, near disasters, and lucky bounces. This is a story about taking the long view and aligning everyone—partners, investors, team members, suppliers, guests, neighbors, friends, and family around the power of partnerships and patience.

Our journey began when we—Matt, David, and Erik—decided to put a pin in the map of our lives—where we hoped to be and what we hoped to do over the next decade. That "pin" served as our internal GPS—alerting us when we'd taken a wrong turn, sometimes suggesting dangers ahead, and occasionally proposing an alternate route.

We hope our story will encourage you to find your own path. As we like to say, "We're not here to judge you. We're here to nudge you."

LISTEN TO YOUR INNER VOICE

In 2002, we were all working at Shutters on the Beach, a Santa Monica luxury hotel and fine dining destination. David was food and beverage director, Erik was executive chef, and Matt was chef de cuisine of 1 Pico, one of Shutters' signature restaurants.

At the time, David wasn't asking himself a ten-year legacy question. He was wondering how he had arrived at such a low point, working in a job he no longer found rewarding. Worse yet, he felt stuck, alone, unable to confide in anyone, and completely without the tools to help him get out.

It was during an annual performance review when David posed the cliched question to his executive chef, "Erik, where do you see yourself in five years?" Expecting a similarly clichéd response from the chef, David was surprised when Erik said, "Can we have this conversation off the record?" David leaned in.

Since 1996, Erik had been trying to answer a question that came to him every time he waited in line at the wildly popular Pancho Villa taqueria in San Francisco's Mission District. "How can I do something like this with my style of cooking?" When the answer came to him, it seemed quite simple—source the best local ingredients, prepare them skillfully, and sell them at a price most people could afford on a regular basis.

At the time, the restaurant industry in California and in much of the U.S. had an abundance of expensive fine dining, special occasion restaurants where superior ingredients were transformed by highly trained chefs. Erik categorized the 1% served by these elite restaurants as "the newly wed and nearly dead."

At the low end of the industry, fast food and convenience food retailers dominated, providing inexpensive go-to options of unhealthy choices for millions of eaters. To the best of our knowledge, there were no restaurants offering professionally prepared food with high-quality ingredients at an affordable price. This is where Erik sensed opportunity. He drafted a Tender Greens menu and concept statement and took the idea to fellow chef Matt Lyman. Matt saw the potential and was fully on board with the opportunity to create a different kind of dining experience for customers and a better work/life environment for culinary workers. Together, Matt & Erik began developing their shared vision for the Ten Year Plan for Tender Greens.

By answering David's future aspirations question, Erik took a risk. He shared his outline for the Tender Greens concept and the initial conversations he and Matt had been having with potential suppliers. That was a jumping off point for David.

It was the first time he had felt excited about anything in far too long. Really scared, but excited. Two days later, after discussing this with his wife, Randi, he called Erik. "This is exactly how we want to live and we believe others do too. I would like to help you build this."

BE ALL IN

From the beginning, we agreed on the underlying values that would define Tender Greens: A locally based supply chain with suppliers as equity partners. A company culture that nurtures people. A brand that customers love. A holistic business that benefits all stakeholders.

What each of us felt at this mid-stage of our careers was like having a splinter lodged in us—nagging us to do something that fed our passions and purpose. It's what brought us together over Tender Greens.

We started holding early morning secret meetings at our "international HQ," the local Peet's Coffee. We'd organize our side hustle activities and divvy up projects before heading in to work. At times, we'd meet on the boardwalk, not very clandestinely since Erik was in chefs' whites and we stuck out like sore thumbs. Once the partnership was formed in this private way, when we'd see each other going about our jobs at Shutters, it was like the bond of belonging to a secret society—we knew something that no one else did.

David soon felt the pull to leave his demanding role as food and beverage director, enabling him to devote more time to Tender Greens. In 2003, to pay the bills, he took a job as a pool server at the five-star Peninsula Hotel in Beverly Hills. Quite a comedown in pay and professional prestige. But it gave him more time and energy to work on Tender Greens. It also meant that two consecutive days of rain could mean personal financial disaster.

Erik and Matt continued to work at Shutters on the Beach, getting regular paychecks and using their positions to bolster their street credibility and to conduct R&D on behalf of Tender Greens. They used menu specials to test and perfect potential Tender Greens recipes. During down times, they simulated kitchen and dining room layouts, moving tables and chairs around the empty ballroom—like the scene in the film "The Founder" when Ray Kroc uses a basketball court to simulate how to lay out a McDonald's kitchen to optimize efficiency.

This arrangement might have been painless had it lasted for the few months we optimistically predicted. Instead, it stretched on for what began to seem like an eternity. We incorporated as T.Y.P. Restaurant Group, Inc. in 2004. Capital raising went on in earnest from 2004 through 2005. We still struggled to refine our business plan, raise initial capital, and do the million other tasks required to launch a business. From that initial conversation between Erik and David, nearly four years passed before the grand opening of the first Tender Greens.

IT TAKES LONGER THAN YOU THINK

An early test of endurance came during the limbo period of 2003-2005. David was called for jury duty on a plaintiff case demanding damages for emotional trauma caused by a Mercedes SUV stalling on the 405 freeway. The case dragged on for several excruciating days. Instead of pulling down tips at the Peninsula, David earned $11 per diem jury pay. On his lunch break one day, he cashed in some of his 401(k) to pay his mortgage.

To many of his colleagues and acquaintances, David may have looked like a courageous maverick. In reality, this was an extremely stressful time. It surely proved beyond a doubt that David had real skin in the game. Failure would have meant the unthinkable. Going back to past jobs or applying for another hospitality management position were options too wretched to consider. The high stakes generated high motivation. This idea simply had to work.

While Matt and Erik didn't share David's financial stress, they were carrying the burden of holding down two jobs—their full-time chef positions and the relentless demands of the start-up side hustle.

These long years challenged us as individuals and as partners to understand what we wanted to accomplish. It's one thing to kick around an idea and have some speculative conversations— those after-hours wine words or tequila talks fantasizing about "Wouldn't it be cool if...?" What separates dreamers from visionaries is what happens next.

Dreamers never get past the ideation stage, generating reams of great ideas that never materialize. Visionaries start with what is real, see beyond to what's possible, then do the hard work to make it happen.

All the effort in this early stage revealed who we were. How hard we were willing to work. What we would sacrifice. Where we wouldn't compromise. The early times tested us to live our values. It reassured us we were aligned and equally committed. The strength of our partnership and our belief in each other is what kept us going.

If any of us had tried this as a solo venture, it would have been easy to give up as the setbacks and disappointments piled up. But we couldn't let each other down, so we kept finding the energy to persevere. We had firmly planted our "pin in the map."

Chapter 2

The Heavy Lift from Idea to Business: Forming the T.Y.P. Restaurant Group

"Know what you bring. Know what you don't bring. And build a team that covers everything you need."
– Angie Hicks

*W*riting a description of a business concept and laying out a vision grounded in long-held principles is the easy part. Much harder is developing a detailed business plan, especially when you're trying to create a wholly new product, service, or business model. How do you get feedback without risking exposure? Where are you likely to find allies or essential information? Our journey from idea to business held some surprises and unexpected supporters.

INVESTING IN A SOLID BUSINESS PLAN IS WORTH IT

In the excitement of our early days, we shared the idea of Tender Greens and our deeply held ideals with each other. We talked about people we admired like John Mackey from Whole Foods and Howard Schultz at Starbucks—Mackey's notion of "conscious capitalism" that meant win-win for everyone the business touches, and Schultz's commitment to creating a workplace with dignity and opportunity. We named the people in the industry we wanted to emulate and those we did not want to end up like. We wanted to incorporate all the good stuff from our collective decades of experience. And we vowed never to imitate the bad stuff we had all witnessed in the restaurant business. This exercise helped us identify our ideals.

These conversations helped us clarify what we wanted to accomplish beyond making money. We were able to visualize what we wanted our company culture to be like for us and for the people who would help us create a legacy brand. We would be looking for people who needed something beyond a stable job—individuals seeking something to connect with and take pride in, who shared our values and our vision of the world, and our role in shaping it. We made this clear when we invited people to join the journey. At the time, this approach was rare. In today's business landscape, not defining your brand with clearly articulated values is a serious misstep.

As crucial as our philosophical conversations were, if we were going to get anywhere with Tender Greens we needed to move past ideals to concrete plans. The menu and supply chain-based concept Erik and Matt had developed was the beginning. The original outline answered some questions but didn't answer them all. It needed a lot more specificity. It needed to be structured in a way that would speak to investors. And it definitely needed a defined offering.

David used that outline as the foundation for a business plan, conceived in tandem with a project management document. The plan addressed everything we wanted to achieve. The project timelines laid out when things had to happen in order to hit important milestones.

Roughly, the steps we followed chronologically were:

- Define and refine the idea.
- Use the business planning process to identify gaps.
- Get very clear on our partnership agreement.
- Figure out finances, both personal and professional.
- Construct a detailed critical path to opening day.
- Identify and recruit stakeholders.
- Commit to evolving all plans through continuous learning.

We're big advocates of airing all the pros and cons of business plans. Done diligently, a business plan forces you to hash out the variables. It fleshes out what your business, product, or service will look, taste, and feel like. It compels you to find solutions to how you're going to make, sell, and distribute it.

A thoughtful plan digs up where the landmines are hidden, including the inevitable gaping holes in your skill set. In partnerships, it should surface disagreements on fundamental things like pricing, marketing, and HR issues. Done well, the business plan enables you to launch your enterprise with as much grace as possible. Most importantly, a well-considered business plan becomes a statement of concepts and values that aligns everyone around a common language.

Once you know what skills and qualities are needed for your particular business, you can honestly assess how many of them you can profess to have covered. A key to successful partnerships is to find complementary people. Too much sameness and you're not covering all the necessary skills a business requires. What brought the three of us together were the things we're each good at. Erik and Matt were talented, well-connected chefs. While Erik may have been a bit romantic in his connection to food, Matt was a pragmatist—a great technician with a reliable palette and an engineer's mind for creating effective systems. David was an excellent trainer and operations manager. We didn't know much about writing business plans, but collectively we had more than forty years of industry knowledge to build a plan on.

We bought some software, started writing a detailed plan, and drew up a list of potential investors. Throughout the process, we had to humbly face that we were not sufficiently prepared for many of the business issues beyond restaurant operations: investor documentation, presentations, legal entity formation, GAAP accounting, HR details, permitting, and construction to name a few. This was a valuable realization because it forced us to supplement our plan early through research and learning.

We relentlessly revised the business model so that once we raised enough money we could start quickly. Erik and Matt kept testing specials and kitchen configurations at Shutters to "engineer the menu." David was in charge of keeping track of where we were in the project timeline and what needed to happen next.

The discipline of a side hustle helps you mitigate some of the potential for failure. You commit to looking squarely at all the gray areas, all the black holes of unknowns that can be anticipated. Then you do what it takes to figure out plausible solutions you can all accept. We tried to do as much as possible under the protection of this planning stage. It was what happily woke us up at 4 a.m. to work on before going to our paying gigs.

Our practice of continual scenario building had another clear end goal—we were honing the concept so we could convince people to lend us money. Though none of us had gone after investors before, we knew we had to have a sound pitch and package before anyone would write a check.

BUSINESS FIRST. PARTNERS SECOND. FRIENDS THIRD

While we still had our regular paychecks, we weren't fully committed; we were emotionally on board, but we weren't base jumping yet. There comes a point when you have to pull the cord and go for it. The reality is that things will get very uncomfortable—it'll feel like you've jumped off a cliff. For us, it was safer to take the leap with a group of people than attempt it alone.

Once we did, we knew we'd be working eighteen hours a day, seven days a week, so we had to figure out how to function together and make things equitable. We would pay ourselves equally, even schedule ourselves equally. It was fair—and equally bad for everybody.

Having a way to resolve conflict was important to strengthening our partnership. We agreed that the business came first, over personal considerations or friendship. From the beginning, we took advantage of "the power of three." Major decisions would be determined by a 2/3 vote. The odd number of partners ensured we'd never have a stalemate. There would always be somebody to break the occasional tie. Lobbying was permitted, and each of us would often resort to asking another to "take a walk" so he could argue his position separately.

Matt's voice was key in moments of debate between Erik and David. As a chef he could often appreciate Erik's chef-centered perspective when faced with a debatable issue. As a systems engineer he was equally apt to support David's desire to narrow the guardrails for consistency in growth. We often found ourselves working to sway Matt to our side of a debated topic. But in the end, it came down to one man, one vote. It's like having a built-in mediator.

We also agreed to be punctual or to call ahead proactively, and to bring our grievances to each other rather than to others in our organization, and never to complain down the line. We would hold each other accountable first and encourage others to do the same. It was essential to honor the commitments we made, and to respect and support each other's time off as much as possible.

Early on, we decided to operate like a mature company even when we were just getting started. We imitated some of the professionalism and structure of the larger companies we had worked for as a foundation to build our business on. This meant adopting professional systems as opposed to winging it with a pad of paper and a pencil. In addition, we began by defining our standards closely tied to our values. This professional attitude helped our success by shaping our food and our culture. It protected us from the slippery slope of making decisions under duress that might lead us away from the high bar we had set for ourselves. We committed to always striving to be "special" as a way to guard against the downward creep of quality migration.

Although it happened many years later, the controversy over paper napkins illustrates what happens when your values are woven into your culture. In the ongoing effort to trim costs, we brought in lower quality paper napkins at significant savings. This was a noticeable departure from our insistence on the best of everything. But how important were napkins to the Tender Greens customer experience? Nobody came for the napkins, right? We were economizing but also believed that a switch away from baskets of napkins to napkin dispensers would be better for the planet—people would take only what they needed instead of grabbing a wasteful handful from the open baskets.

Our staff rebelled. We heard first from our regional manager in LA. "The teams don't believe that these dispensed napkins are better for people or the planet." Complaints surfaced from other locations as well. It wasn't as if our team members organized a work slowdown or walked out, but they were vocal in reminding us that our job was "to operate restaurants that people really loved." And nobody loved our "cheap-ass paper napkins."

They were right. Even our "save the planet" argument didn't hold up, because guests ended up taking more of the flimsy napkins. Better paper napkins prevailed. Being challenged by our staff wasn't the greatest feeling. But because their uprising was rooted in our company values, we appreciated being held accountable. Our team members did the right thing in speaking up and pushing back; our values were being honored even if we were being embarrassed.

As a new business, we benefited from having close collaborators whom we could trust and who would challenge us. No one has all the answers. We were all highly opinionated about different things, including things we didn't know much about! But we understood and respected what each one brought to the business.

Our partnership, founded on the premise of equality, required that we take turns and play different roles. The analogy we used was a jazz trio. Everybody gets to solo with riffs and backup from the others. We each needed somebody to cheer us on, dig us out of the occasional slumps, and celebrate the small wins. And to let us shine at what we did best. Our partnership agreement formalized our commitment to parity while recognizing our unique strengths.

GET FEEDBACK FROM PEOPLE YOU TRUST

As an entrepreneur, you've got this idea that is evolving into a detailed plan. How do you test it? Whom can you trust not to steal your idea and run with it? This is scary stuff, yet essential to consider. David felt paranoid about starting to talk openly about the plan but took some comfort in the fact that what we were trying to do was so difficult, it would be crazy for anyone else to try it.

We began talking to people who could help us on our mission. Our pitch wasn't fully polished but it was full of integrity. We were foodies excited about a new, authentic idea—not dentists who were sick of being dentists and thought starting a restaurant would be fun. We wanted to bring something really delicious to market that people would crave and could afford. We wanted everything about the company to be different and cool. There was nothing like it at the time.

Some of these encounters were random opportunities. One day, David's general manager at the Peninsula Hotel was having lunch with Starbucks CEO Howard Schultz. The GM tossed David a softball, telling Schultz that David was "working on an idea." David launched into his spiel. Schultz listened and said, "Go for it. Don't quit." It's hard to quantify how much that encouragement meant. We were getting positive reactions from other people in the business, but this was like hearing from the oracle.

We learned from experiences like this. David, something of a perfectionist, worked on his pitch after every encounter. Each positive response buoyed us a little and emboldened us to extend our outreach.

Building a strong, affordable supply chain was crucial to our business model. We began creating it by sounding out reputable suppliers with whom we had existing relationships, most notably Scarborough Farms, Village Imports, and Breadworks. We asked for their insights, advice, and buy-in. We invited them in as our partners, not simply as vendors working transactions for fees. We offered privileged deals to a handful of premier companies who would turn out to be equity partners. In return, we asked for confidential and favorable terms. We were highly selective and muted around these deals and so were our new partners. Our supply chain began to take shape.

In this busy pre-launch time, optimism and our conviction that we were working toward a higher purpose fueled our efforts. We loved testing dishes for the menu, catering small pitch parties to attract potential investor interest, and seeing genuine excitement about the food. Our confidence grew as the business plan got better at anticipating and answering questions from skeptics. Working on the business plan was exciting. Since all the documents were on David's computer, he was doing the updates and sharing them back. His backpack held all our hopes and dreams.

Still, things weren't moving fast enough. No money was coming in yet. There were low moments of drag and doubt—is this ever going to happen? Managing expectations with spouses and families created a lot of tension. Personal distractions threatened internal dysfunction for the partnership.

Together we watched the documentary "Some Kind of Monster," chronicling the rock band Metallica's growing pains and subsequent intervention by Coach Phil Towle just prior to the release of their album, "St. Anger." This movie profoundly marked our partnership as both a harbinger and a lighthouse. The band had to learn how to put their differences aside, quiet the outside distractions, and focus on what was important—their music. It was advice we committed to follow for Tender Greens.

People were giving us good feedback and even some attaboys. But we needed more than that. We sounded out a wider circle of people. We listened. We adapted our plan. Suddenly our idea was now a *thing*. We started forming new relationships, getting broader interest, and as part of the process, developing a much more refined pitch deck. That felt good because we were really into it, and almost ready to do the ultimate heavy lift: raise significant capital.

Chapter 3

Raising Capital: Financial, Intellectual, and Human

"Good values are like a magnet – they attract good people."
–*John Wooden*

A working definition of "entrepreneur" is someone who believes they can accomplish their goals despite obvious shortfalls of assets— whether it's capital, knowledge, or networks. This chapter describes how we came to terms with the founder's dilemma—what you know, what you don't, and how to fill in the gaps.

BUILD YOUR VALUES INTO YOUR BUSINESS PLAN

When we felt we had enough clarity about our concept to start discussing it with other people, we took it first to those we believed would be a friendly audience—our network of suppliers. This was a critical strategic move. Our values dictated that we would always select local over national food providers. Our goal of making good food affordable at scale meant we had to have preferential pricing and long-term commitments.

Our business model depended on approaching our capital raise and the creation of our supply chain as a package. Our aim was to invite every substantial entity in our supply chain to be an equity partner. With the values-aligned suppliers we identified, we proposed investment. We were delighted when they chose to participate.

True partnership was the motivation behind our approach. We wanted to have confidence and control over the supply chain, but we're not farmers, importers, or purveyors of food. We partnered with those who are experts and gave them equity in exchange for their willingness to match our commitment to patient growth. Key to Tender Greens' success was forming a long-view relationship that was mutually beneficial and also provided short-term value. In business terms, we achieved vertical integration through partnerships with suppliers.

It's the difference between working with a vendor versus an equity partner. In a purely transactional vendor relationship, if it stops working even for the short term because of shifting economics or business disruptions, that relationship is at risk. One side starts to squeeze the other or feel exploited. By bringing our suppliers in as equity partners, we aimed to set a long-view relationship that was strong enough to endure any short-term disruption.

When inevitable business stresses would occur, Tender Greens would get preference. Any issues in the macro economy—oil price hikes; escalating trucking, labor, or packaging costs; product shortages due to drought—when both parties are bonded in equity, the relationship has resilience. The suppliers are going to shoulder the short-term pain to get you through because in the long term, they will reap the reward. Similarly, we pledged to stick with a farm or purveyor even if they were having temporary trouble meeting their obligations to us.

This business model resulted from having seen bad things happen in many of our previous restaurant experiences. As David knew from managing food and beverage operations at luxury properties, traditional thinking dictates that you can often just increase prices to cover rising costs—gouge your guests. Or you can pressure your vendors to reduce their prices to shrink their small margins even further—squeeze your suppliers. As a large, lucrative account, you can dictate the terms especially for smaller suppliers who feel they can't afford to lose your business. That's how farmers end up with cents on the dollar for their products.

In our experience, we had all witnessed unsustainable pressures placed on the supply chain to protect or expand our employer's margins. For Tender Greens we aimed to preserve margins for everyone while delivering value to our guests. This was a goal best achieved through partnerships of shared risk and reward. We wanted a sustainable supply chain model that benefited everybody participating in it. If you're just squeezing the supply chain, it's not sustainable. And it surely doesn't align with our identity.

Founder-led companies whose products and conduct we admired were where we began our pitch. We recognize this approach isn't foolproof. We made some bad picks. And sometimes the relationships changed over time and no longer worked.

What we learned were ways to find our ideal partners, those who were able to envision and appreciate the potential for shared value creation. Often we opened with the admission, "Our concept is based on affordable customer pricing and to make that work we can't really afford your products." But we'd go on to explain our goal of "democratizing good food" and our plans for scale. We'd discuss an approach to preferential pricing based on growing together, confident that the volume we'd be able to buy would justify the price. Then we posed the question, "What do you think about partnering with us?"

In our pitch, we were selling a vision of what Tender Greens and the supplier could do together. Greater growth, stronger brand integrity, and larger profits than either of us could do alone. And high-quality ingredients being enjoyed by more consumers.

Smart suppliers see the limits of their own enterprise. We were offering a stake in what we intended to be a growth brand. There were going to be some risks, though our partnership would do our best to mitigate those. The promise was that we'd all make some money along the journey and there'd be a bonus at the end of our Ten Year Plan.

WRITE YOUR PLAN WITH THE READER IN MIND

Going out to meet with investors didn't start in earnest until David left his role at Shutters on the Beach in 2003. We started with industry insiders like suppliers where we knew our professional credibility was in place.

As we ventured outside that group into the larger business community, we got tougher questions. The pushback we heard on some elements of our business plan showed us what we were absolute about. Questions about or objections to our plan surfaced in areas where we weren't going to budge. However, input from the business community also showed where we were uncertain or under-informed. When these gaps emerged, we were receptive to refining our thinking based on smart feedback.

Very importantly, we took a second look at advertising and marketing—admittedly, we weren't marketing-minded and our plan didn't have a clear approach. We knew we wanted to avoid anything gimmicky like discounts. In a pre-social media marketing world, the options were very different. "Guerilla" marketing got our attention. We adopted the tactic of taking part in chef-driven, high-end food events as a starting place to create buzz and PR.

Meanwhile our locations site criteria and site selection process were lacking detailed thought. We needed to be much clearer on which qualities would make a location a sound business decision.

Risk mitigation or governance concerns surfaced from potential investors. In our idealistic view, we weren't thinking about "running off with the money." But before money people would take us seriously, we had to answer their need for assurances. We developed banking, financial oversight, and detailed HR policies. In short, we demonstrated accountability for the claims we were making that promised ethical business operations. Hearing from these multiple, pragmatic perspectives enabled us to develop a richer narrative for Tender Greens, one that could speak to more sophisticated potential investors.

This was an interesting process. It strengthened our core values and educated us. With each pitch, we did more research, refined our model, and grew more skilled in our speaking parts, especially how and when to riff off each other.

Still, there were times we felt sorry for ourselves. It was taking too long to find the money we needed. We didn't have easy access to lots of capital. The "friends and family" route so many entrepreneurs start with enabled us to raise critical initial funds. However, not many from our close circle had the additional resources to re-up for the ensuing larger capital raises.

Having to look beyond "true believers" made us better at selling Tender Greens. We had to earn that capital by anticipating where our plan was vulnerable. Refining the plan and pitching the business to investors was frustrating but exciting, especially when we started to see money flow in.

As grateful as we were to those who wrote checks for this initial capital, we were also anxious about protecting their investment.

A friend arranged to have our business plan reviewed by a faculty member at Harvard Business School! We got very positive feedback and that gave us a significant confidence boost.

PARTNERSHIPS BUILD EQUITY

Although he's not sure who said this, one bit of wisdom stayed with Erik from this period: "If you want advice, ask for money. If you want money, ask for advice."

By 2004, we had exhausted much of our friends and family network. Beyond that inner circle, we had some professional relationships with value-added money. Blending our approach of raising money with identifying supply chain partners gave us our first substantial pledge of capital.

Scarborough Farms, a family farm in operation since 1986, had long served some of the top fine dining restaurants in California. Owner Ann Stein and her family enjoyed a stellar reputation for sustainably growing consistently flavorful, beautiful, unique produce. They were respected for their products and valued for their pledge to deliver dependable, high-quality service to chefs and restaurants. Tender Greens needed a produce supplier of this quality. Scarborough was the first supplier we approached with an offer of equity partnership.

Because Erik had been buying from Scarborough for many years, trust was already in place. When he laid out the concept for Tender Greens and sketched the idea of a partnership, Ann's first response was, "We've been waiting for someone to make us an offer like this."

Despite this promising start, we had a long way to go to make a solid deal. Many conversations ensued. Months went by. Multiple times the partnership almost got torpedoed by one anxiety or another.

Finally, we arrived at an agreement enabling Tender Greens to receive product in trade and a capital infusion of $150,000. Our initial offering was structured as a Min/Max of $900,000, so this deal was a landmark. Happily, our arrangement worked as planned. Scarborough grew with us. We weathered a lot of bumps together. When we exited, the Stein family's patient capital and committed partnership was rewarded and we were proud of being able to honor our promise to them.

Another early influential equity partner was Daniel Nollinger, founder of Village Imports. Like Scarborough, Village Imports served the most discerning high-end restaurant chefs. An importer of premium prepared foods, Daniel had the best oils, vinegars, and culinary staples. He was a respected businessman, a persuasive personality, and a certified food lover. Being French was a bonus.

Just as with Scarborough, we wanted Daniel's products but couldn't afford them at regular wholesale. So we offered him the same sort of deal—an investment opportunity as part of a package of preferential pricing and guaranteed service over the long term. Village Imports signed on with us. In many ways, Daniel delivered far more than prepared foods to us over the years. He became an advocate and ambassador for Tender Greens, spreading the word through his broad professional network.

Seth Silverman was another early believer and enthusiastic backer. We first met Seth at La Brea Bakery in Los Angeles. As we were gearing up to begin Tender Greens, he was moving on from La Brea to run his own bakery, Breadworks. Our businesses were a natural fit. We were proud to have Seth join us as a supplier and an investor.

On a founder-to-founder basis, we could negotiate unique deals that worked for both parties. Trying this same approach with company hierarchies and multiple management levels posed too many obstacles to overcome. We were most successful with owner-led companies who had the desire and ability to grow with us.

Around this time, we were being introduced to more sophisticated investors outside the industry. We had to professionalize our pitch beyond the business plan and our reputations. Erik put on his '90s "vintage" olive green Armani suit dating from his Four Seasons days in Philly, prompting much good-natured "trash talking" from David and Matt. After decades in chef's whites, it was Erik's only good suit. A little partner ridicule was a small price to pay when we were actively seeking significant investors.

Pretty quickly, we discovered it was harder to get these serious money folks to commit. From their perspective, we were still pitching an idea that had never been tried in an industry with a 95% failure rate.

We were fortunate to meet Dick Gordon, an attorney who had done the original offering documents for California Pizza Kitchen. On a semi-pro bono basis, Dick helped us develop our first fully professional offering memo. We had been asking for money and getting advice. But Dick helped change that.

We're very grateful to Tom Jermain, one of our first individual investors. We banked his $25,000 thinking we were on a roll. Instead, from there it was dribs and drabs.

Our capital raising efforts stalled for a long time. This frustrating sense of inertia prompted a series of partner meetings at Westside LA dive bars like The Lost & Found and The Daily Pint—places serving Miller High Life, filled with smokers listening to The Smiths music. We went to places where we knew we wouldn't bump into anybody. These grim backdrops were what we needed, the melodramatic setting for these hard conversations. The ground we kept going over was something like this: "If we hate our jobs and prospects as much as we say we do, if we believe in this new business as much as we say, we have to keep at it." This was our main motivation to keep pushing our pitch despite the many rejections.

Slowly, more people started to write checks. We had about $110,000 in cash investments committed. We were collecting on these pledges and our bank account was growing.

Thinking it was worth exploring, we had our first encounter with professional equity investors. A venture capital firm we'd been introduced to invited us to a meeting on the top floor of a twenty-story office tower. Suited up, Erik still sporting the olive green Armani, and business plan in hand, we walked into the classic, intimidating power boardroom.

The equity partner had read our business plan and let us run through our pitch deck. Within minutes, he explained that if he were to take a position, he would assume control and bring in "his guys from Chicago" to run it. He might retain us; he'd have to take a closer look at that. In less time than it took to ride the elevator to his office, we were being separated from our idea before it was even a functioning business. On the elevator ride down, we were close to throwing up. It would be years before we took another meeting with anyone from private equity.

Since we felt that route wasn't open to us, we looked over our list of prospects and saw we were at an end. That is, except for one personal connection of David's whom he had been reluctant to approach. David's father-in-law could afford to invest, but it ran the risk of complicating the deal and David's family life. Letting business and investment risk come between them just seemed unwise. However, the bank statement didn't lie. We needed one more substantial investor, one more significant chunk of money to finish our capital drive. Only then could we sign a lease. Without it, we may as well start refunding deposits.

Erik had a heart-to-heart with David. "This is our best hope for funding the startup. Maybe our last hope. Would it help if I went with you?" We pulled out our best dog-and-pony show routine and pitched to David's father-in-law. It worked. By 2005, we were finally able to sign our first lease.

We'd managed to secure the foundational capital for our business with our values intact. Through equity partner deals, most of our produce and specialty prepared foods were assured.

Often early-stage founders refuse to consider parting with any equity. What we experienced with Tender Greens was the exponential value of trading equity judiciously. As founders you can have 100% of something small or a smaller percentage of something huge. What made our business possible was surrounding ourselves with people who were able to help us get what we needed. We were distributing equity appropriately for what these partnerships could and did deliver in the short and long term.

The downside of the equity partnerships we formed with suppliers is that they are really good until they're not. In a straight vendor relationship, you can fire each other. In an equity partner relationship, it is more complicated. We learned over time to build contingencies and complexity into the partnership agreements. Building in protections to cover death, inability to fulfill responsibilities, and other unanticipated events proved to be the smart solution.

While we always looked for win-win outcomes, what started out as back-of-the-napkin-style agreements later got tightened up by lawyers. Handshake deals might seem appealing but aren't useful even on the upside. As we saw how much effort and energy it took to manage these partnerships, we came to realize the value of having every relationship memorialized by a lawyer who shared our values, not a well-intentioned but inexperienced uncle or friend.

When we set it up right, our contract provided protection against what can be devastating fluctuations in price, quality, availability, dependability. Our suppliers had confidence to expand because our side of the deal offered them a predictable end user, fair prices, and the ability to grow in a forecasted way. Our suppliers boosted their credibility on the claim, "We sell to Tender Greens." Both parties benefited from the powerful marketing value that results when we could tell the story of true partnership.

As we've seen in national food safety scares, there is also tremendous value in having full transparency in the supply chain. If there was a problem in a commodity—an outbreak that resulted in a national food scare—we were in a protected position because we knew where our food came from. Not off a truck from a warehouse that aggregates products from multiple growers.

When spinach was disappearing from U.S. restaurants and grocery shelves after an *E. coli* outbreak, Tender Greens was featured on "Nightline" because our service was uninterrupted. We could continue confidently selling our salads because we knew exactly who was growing our food.

In some cases an investor's supply company did not grow with Tender Greens. Sometimes our growth outpaced theirs or their business practices no longer meshed with ours. We continued our investor relationship, though we stopped buying from them as a supplier.

We close out this period of Tender Greens as a time of massive learning for us. We had gone far beyond ourselves and our circle to gather all kinds of necessary capital—financial, intellectual, and human. The drive to acquire investors also increased our store of intellectual capital from the advice of seasoned businesspeople. Human capital came in the form of the many new relationships we built with suppliers, investors, and business professionals.

We were growing rich in some ways, but for each of us these were financially lean days with many more lean years to come. We paid ourselves what we could and nothing more. We were putting every layer of skin into the game. People thought we were doing quite well—and we were from a business perspective—but it was the beginning of many years of personal financial struggle. What carried us was the belief that Tender Greens ultimately would succeed.

Chapter 4

Details Matter: Opening Day

"There is no certainty; there is only adventure."
–*Roberto Assagioli*

USE EVERY AVAILABLE RESOURCE, INCLUDING OUTSIDE HELP

*O*ur first location, Culver City, nearly met our full list of site selection criteria. It had an enormous patio, cute interior, plentiful street parking, easy ingress and egress, and attractive frontage in an up-and-coming area. It was adjacent to a dense daytime office population and was supported at night by a bedroom community. And we could afford the rent. We wanted Tender Greens to be a genuine neighborhood restaurant, not a bland façade in a SoCal strip mall. We looked at dozens of locations and this neighborhood felt right. The only thing missing was the landlord's approval. She wanted a sushi bar. She wanted a sure thing. She definitely did not want an unproven startup.

We tried to win her over, inundating her with every argument we could conjure. When those failed, we unleashed our secret weapon—investor, true believer, and founder of Village Imports, Daniel Nollinger.

Daniel breezed into the landlord's office in tennis shorts and Lacoste shirt, looking more prepared for a game of doubles than for a lease negotiation. As a successful businessman, Daniel had street cred. As a Frenchman passionate about high-quality food, he had irresistible charm. He told the landlord why he was personally invested in Tender Greens and why we'd be perfect for her building. "These guys have what it takes to be a big success," he said. "Wouldn't you like your property to be the flagship location for a wildly popular restaurant brand?" Daniel was 100% pure cheerleading ambassador for Tender Greens. He impressed her. We got our lease agreement. Erik and Matt gave notice that they were leaving Shutters.

One major hurdle behind us—a massive number of them still ahead. We remember this time as exhilarating. We were working through our project timelines, making decisions as a trio, calling the shots the way we thought best, being accountable to ourselves. It all felt really great, except for the dwindling bank account. We were anxiously aware that there would be no more money coming in until we got the restaurant doors open.

We were learning our lesson about being beholden to the city and to subcontractors. We had been "Robin Hooding" this project to save money, cutting deals for trade, and doing lots of the demolition and construction work ourselves. Steve Haigh, an early investor, generously served as acting general contractor. He found materials and reliable subcontractors for us that kept the project moving. We're forever grateful for Steve's commitment to our success.

The space where we planned to build the large, open kitchen—a radical idea at the time and a key component of our design plan— was completely unfinished. It had a dirt floor, no lights, and no plumbing. We weren't builders but we could read construction plans. We knew we needed plumbing and that plumbing required trenches. The plans called for 18-inch deep troughs, so we dug them. We poured the concrete foundation for the walk-in cooler. We built the light fixtures from 2x6's and track lighting.

The place was starting to come together. One afternoon, David and Matt were taking a break on the roof when they heard a terrible noise. They watched the tarpaper of the roof suddenly bulge, accompanied by a sickening ripping sound. A beam that had been resting on a forklift fell off, taking with it all the ceiling wiring and leaving a gaping hole in the roof. One more unexpected repair, delay, expense.

Then came the failed safety inspection. Those slick track lights we'd built from stuff we got at Home Depot looked awesome. The safety inspector had a different perspective. "You don't have any earthquake protection on those lights. What's going to keep them anchored to the ceiling in a quake?" David didn't have an answer but told the inspector they'd get it figured out in time for a re-inspection the next day. The only thing David had ever seen anchored to a ceiling was a ceiling fan, so he went to Home Depot, charged six ceiling fans to his close-to-maxed out credit card, lugged the boxes to his car, took out the six mounts, taped the boxes shut and returned them. Problem solved. Zero cost. Safety inspection passed.

We're not sharing this story because we're proud of such a dodgy move. We share it to show how desperate we were to get the doors open. For months, money had been flowing out. We needed it to start flowing in. By way of making amends to Home Depot, we purchased thousands of dollars of construction materials over the coming years, paying full price. We like to think they'd forgive us for this "Robin Hood" move in our early days.

Since money was unbelievably tight, we repurposed or reused everything we could. The previous tenant had installed two handsome wooden French doors with glass panels. They were great looking, but not right for the Tender Greens style. Matt and David stripped them, sealed them, and used leftover sections of beams to make legs for two desks. One of our investors, Bernard Lax, owned an industrial glass company and offered to make custom glass desktops to cover the recessed door panels. These became our office desks. They are still in the Tender Greens offices today.

Even with our hands-on approach and detailed project timeline, we were learning that it's one thing to have your plans laid out. But when we failed an inspection or our subcontractors weren't available, we found ourselves stuck waiting. Also waiting were the staff we'd already hired, wondering when their jobs were going to start. And all the time we fixated on our money evaporating. That $900,000 we'd secured to open our first three restaurants was now down to $850. Instead of three stores built out, we had one restaurant—as yet unopened.

HOPE FOR THE BEST; PLAN FOR THE WORST. BUT PLAN FOR THE BEST TOO

Finally in 2006, the June day arrived when the construction barriers out front could be taken down.

One thing we prized about our first location was the huge jacaranda tree in front. This tropical beauty is a stunning sight in bloom, covered in spectacular lavender blossoms. The flowers are gorgeous on the tree, but a mess on the sidewalk. On opening day, David went out around 8 a.m. to sweep the walk as staff were arriving to prep and set up. We were insanely happy, busy making sure we had everything looking just right, the staff primed for service and the menu fresh and ready to go. We planned for a lovely day serving delicious food to whoever showed up.

Twenty minutes before the doors opened at 11:30 a.m., David took a broom outside for a last sweeping. There were people waiting in line. Many people. In fact, they formed a line that went down the block and around the corner. We were officially open for business.

It was a crazy day. Everything we anticipated happened, but at a dizzyingly accelerated pace. And naturally some things we didn't plan for happened too.

Customers flooded the restaurant and were immediately caught up in the Tender Greens experience. Although it is commonplace now, when we opened it was novel to have the kitchen fully exposed to guests. Our concept had guests view a wall-mounted menu, verbally place their order with the cook at the top of the kitchen line, then walk the length of the kitchen so they could watch their food being made. When they arrived at the cash register, they'd get their drinks, tell the cashier what they ordered, and settle their tab as their food magically appeared. A fine process for leisurely service, but a hot mess with a line out the door. We didn't have a computer at the door because we couldn't afford one and didn't think we'd need it. People had to remember what they ordered to tell the cashier. That's great until you have a dad ordering for five family members and getting flummoxed at the cash register.

The exposed kitchen meant we had no place to hide as things got frantic. Our steak plate consisted of grilling flat iron steaks, resting them for a few minutes before slicing and plating them. We remember the grill cooks rushing to fill orders, slicing juicy steaks right off the grill leaving so much blood on the cutting board that the station looked like a crime scene. But guests seemed so delighted by the newness, the freshness, and the deliciousness that they were very forgiving.

From a design perspective, we learned fast about building for appropriate capacity and maximum utility. Just about everything we had was too small—soup pots, undercounter dishwasher, a home kitchen-sized ice machine. Artsy green aprons with big wooden buttons that had to be dry cleaned. Little cheffy touches like a display of Erik's elegant Japanese knives and cutting board that were quickly swept into a bucket, making room for more service area.

Our first day ended early. We closed at 7:30 p.m. for the simple reason that we ran out of food. We didn't have a night cleaning crew so we sent the staff home and set about cleaning up the wreckage. It was the first time—but it wouldn't be the last—that we partners divvied up the closeout chores. Erik remembers finding David in the back alley, hosing down funky floor mats, soaked to the neck in grease and dirty water. David remembers Erik losing his footing while mopping and squeegeeing the kitchen floor. His forehead grazed one of the stainless pegs holding the cutting boards to the salad tops, leaving him unaware of the line of blood making its way down his face as he focused on mopping. We were a sorry sight, but we were elated.

It was a baptism by fire for sure, but we had made it through. And for the first time in many months, we could put money *in* the bank. We had a ragtag team of enthusiastic staff. What we didn't have was any idea how popular we were going to be right off the bat. It was a good start. Despite our careful planning, we were woefully unprepared to be this successful.

Later we discovered that Tender Greens had been featured opening day in The Daily Candy. Founded in 2000, The Daily Candy was an online media company that produced daily newsletters in many cities, letting readers know about "hip and trendy" events in their locales. An early forerunner of social media, The Daily Candy targeted the sweet spot audience for Tender Greens. Young food enthusiasts showed up in droves, then came back the next day with friends. We never expected that the whole of LA's Westside would find us so fast. Clearly we were on to something.

Having such a strong start is amazing but it's not possible to maintain that pace day in and day out without relief. We were working flat out every day just to keep up. As soon as lunch was over the first task was to clean up the carnage, put it back together, transition from the lunch crew to the dinner shift. There was food to be ordered, prep lists to write, menus to be planned for tomorrow. A dinner service. More orders, staff scheduling, clean up, handling the day's receipts and tomorrow's cash drawers. We'd do all that and then creep home stinky and exhausted, only to wake up at 6 a.m. and do it again.

Still we maintained the discipline to find time every day to review what was working and what wasn't. Crew highs and lows, products good or bad, production issues that had to be fixed. We'd sit down as a trio, maybe over something to eat, list the issues, and ask how are we going to fix that by tomorrow?

There were operational challenges like not being able to make large enough batches of soup, facility shortcomings like not having a refrigerated place to put vats of soup once they'd been cooked. We were buying bags of ice every day to supplement our woefully inadequate icemaker. And we had to admit that while we'd hired a terrific, high-energy bunch of young kids, we needed more professional firepower in the kitchen.

Our kitchen crew was great at following instructions but they were wholly dependent on the chef telling them everything to do. Even with our deep experience and hands-on supervision, we had a lot to figure out. Refining recipes, adjusting production, it was all a work in progress. We were trying to hire people we could afford. Our young line cooks brought enthusiasm to the job but we needed to build their culinary expertise. We needed cooks who were able to stay ahead in perpetual prep mode, like having the water boiling for potatoes well before we ran out of mashed on the serving line.

We still hadn't figured out how to give ourselves a day off, so we were working seven days a week. Like many other issues we faced, we realized we could do whatever we wanted to fix the problem. There was no one to tell us we had to be open every day so we decided to close on Mondays. Of course, missing Mondays meant missing a day's revenues. The best, most sustainable course of action was to keep making money. Eventually we hit on the right formula. One of us would run the store from 7:00 a.m. to closing so the other two could have some time off. It was hard but it wasn't impossible. Because we were cash flow positive, every day was a good day.

These were demanding months as we figured out more and more about the business, how to manage it, and how to keep making things better. We were getting to see our ideas in action and creating the company and culture we wanted. We were fusing our team members into a tribe. We were solidifying our relationship as partners. Tender Greens was following our Ten Year Plan, and it was working, big time.

SAVOR THE SUCCESSES. DOCUMENT AS MUCH AS YOU CAN

When we think back on the early days, the overwhelming feeling is how much fun we had. Why was it fun? Because we were doing this for ourselves in our own spot—no boss to answer to, no one else's rules to obey. We were what we hoped to be—three guys opening a restaurant with great buzz and lines around the block. It was all hugely affirming!

Our business began to act and feel like who we really were—as evidenced by all the pranking and spontaneous fun. Coming out of the strict, buttoned up, by the book, conservative hotel business, this was a tremendous release for us. As partners, we played off each other's personalities—David's OCD and mild paranoia, Erik's cheffy perfectionism, Matt's constant tinkering. We teased each other and the staff, encouraging the kind of harmless rites of passage familiar to many restaurant workers. Inexperienced staff would be told to go over to a neighboring restaurant to borrow the walk-in expander or the sesame seed peeler, only to return to the laughter of their conspiring co-workers. When it was a team member's birthday, we'd kill the music during service and break into a chorus of "Happy Birthday." Customers would sing along. Equal opportunity embarrassment.

Of course, there were stressful times and occasionally staff in tears. If things weren't going well, Erik might shut down the line and huddle everybody up. Show them it needs to look like this, not like that, and urge them to get it together. David sometimes sent cashiers into the alley to have a little cry. It was a busy restaurant and thus at times unavoidably intense. But we worked to keep the environment honest, completely open, and thoroughly human. Sometimes a do-over conversation and an expression of gratitude after the rush was all that was needed.

There's much we can't recall about these crazy first months, but one beautiful memory was our first December holiday party. We'd been open for six months and the business had matured a lot. To celebrate with our team, we closed after lunch. Matt and Erik set up a taco bar in the kitchen. David had a mariachi band in the dining room. Our team members started arriving, some with dates, others with family members and little kids. It's easy to remember how full of joy this day felt. It held a powerful sense of great abundance. A thriving business, a tribe of loyal team members, and business partners who had become friends. We were in it together. Every day was sink or swim, do or die. And when we couldn't laugh, there was always rosé.

These are rich memories. Looking back, we wish we had more pictures. We were so caught up in the now that we didn't give much thought to preserving these early milestones. If we had a do-over, better documentation would definitely be part of the plan. That and professional bookkeeping.

Partnerships and relationships were crucial to our initial success. In bringing Tender Greens from an idea to a business, we were able to execute on the guiding principles we had set for ourselves four years earlier. We had hoped for the best, planned for the worst, but never considered what achieving the best right away would look like.

This first restaurant showed us we could be a trusted employer. That the culture we wanted to build could exist. We learned to raise money and spend it judiciously. We found that spending down to your last $850 is stressful (and not advisable) but survivable.

Opening the Culver City store to great success was our proof of concept. The next challenge was to capitalize on the store as our teaching and learning center. For us as the company leaders, every day was a chance to run a quick SWOT analysis—assessing our Strengths, Weaknesses, Opportunities, and Threats.

We had the freedom to make decisions and act on them in real time. No meetings to sit through, no need to convince senior management. If we thought something was a better idea, we ran with it. If it flopped, we ditched it and tried something else.

Culver City was our living lab. Over the next two years, we used it to build out the company culture, a loyal guest base (some of whom also became dedicated investors), a reliable supply chain, stronger operating systems, and a distinctive, authentic brand image.

Chapter 5

Creating a Culture of Love and Discipline: It Starts with an Authentic Self

"Deep and simple is far more essential than shallow and complex."
— *Mr. Rogers*

*W*e were fortunate to have three highly experienced individuals as co-founders of Tender Greens. Not only did we combine our years of professional skill and knowledge, but we also shared a clear sense of the type of company we wanted to build. Our goal was to create "restaurants people really love." And when we say that we mean not just guests, but everyone who would be touched by Tender Greens— our guests, suppliers, service providers, investors, and, above all, our team members.

While Erik and Matt focused mainly on the daunting lift of building and running daily operations, David worked on the company's culture—carrying out our shared vision for creating the kind of place where we wanted to work. We committed to building a workplace that values its team members, cultivates excellence and compassion, and favors win-win outcomes and "servant" leadership. David's *blend of life and work lessons positioned him to champion our company culture.*

In this chapter, David reflects on what brought him to this work and makes it deeply satisfying, culminating in his role as Tender Greens first Chief People Officer.

CULTURE IS A PRODUCT OF INTENTIONS SUPPORTED BY ACTION

There are perhaps three Cs that give insight into who I am: Canadian, Capricorn, and Compassionate.

I was raised in Montreal by a loving single mom who worked tirelessly to provide for us. Ruthie Dressler is a kind, funny, and generous woman who gives freely, loves deeply, and puts her special imprint on everything she does. She has taught me the value of hard work and the path of loving kindness.

Although she worked three jobs, sending me to summer camp was out of reach. Her demanding work schedule didn't leave a lot of time to spend with a kid home for the summer, so starting at age 8, I boarded a bus for my relatives' hotel in Lake Placid. I can still remember Buzz, the kindly bus driver. Each summer, he would greet me by name, tell my mom he'd look after me, then literally go out of his way to drop me as close as he could to the hotel.

My great-aunt and great-uncle opened the hotel in Lake Placid during the 1950s. Working there was something of a rite of passage for many of my extended family. An uncle and second cousin had gone on to study hospitality in Europe after apprenticing at the hotel, and had successfully pursued hotel careers in Europe and the U.S. One of my uncles, Stan Bromley, was an early role model for me. I remember keeping magazine clippings about him as he rose to prominence in the hotel industry.

Naturally, when I first started working at the hotel I did many menial tasks—pouring coffee, running plates of food, carrying suitcases, and folding towels. At times I could sometimes slip away to go canoeing or swimming. My aunt and uncle did not have children and this was a more adult than family-oriented resort; there were not a lot of kids to hang out with. Mostly I was either on my own or surrounded by adults.

In retrospect, it is sometimes strange for me to recall that I was sent off alone at such a young age. While it's true it wasn't always that much fun, overall it was a powerful experience where I acquired a strong work ethic and resilience. My relatives may not have been the most nurturing caregivers for younger humans, but they had a lot to teach me about hospitality and fundamental life skills. I quickly came to understand the importance of being there for the guests, being detail oriented, and genuinely caring. I learned how to manage money, deposit my earnings, and save for things I wanted. This was also my introduction to what it feels like to be alienated by work. I was learning the skills of the trade, but not the psycho-emotional elements that contribute to a happy, balanced work environment.

My Lake Placid summer hotel job came to an end when, at age 16, I won a scholarship to travel to Israel for the summer as part of a social experiment bringing together Israeli, Arab, and North American teenagers. This was my first multi-cultural exposure on a peer-to-peer level. It made me hungry to experience more of the cultural richness of the world.

As my uncles had before me, at age 18 I enrolled in the four-year Swiss National Hotel School in Lausanne, Switzerland. The curriculum included co-op placements in various European hotels and restaurants. I was being steeped in the art of classic European hospitality under very strict direction, but that rigidity never really made sense or worked for me. Some of my closest friends at school were kind of revolutionary. We started an underground newspaper, for example, to vent our criticism of the school.

For me this was a time of tremendous personal growth. Many of my school friends were European. On school holidays, I often accompanied them to their family homes. During my time at school, I not only experienced much of Europe, but parts of North Africa and Asia. My training was in luxury settings, but I often traveled to very poor rural regions. Seeing places where people were struggling opened me up to various standards of living and introduced me to the concept of compassion. At an impressionable time of my life, I was exposed to other cultures and different ways of thinking, acting, and feeling.

This early contact with empathy and an awareness that we're not all the same came in handy when we opened our first Tender Greens. Our crew was a diverse group of young kids, many from challenging life circumstances. I'd been a latchkey kid from a single parent household; I knew how hard it is to be a parent and how hard it is to be a kid in that world. It came naturally to have compassion for our young team members from that environment, for those being raised by grandparents, for those who had experienced homelessness, and for those crisscrossing Los Angeles to work two or three jobs to support their own kids.

When I finished my studies in Switzerland, I moved to California to take a position with Hyatt. My next career move was to New York City where I joined the opening team for the Four Seasons hotel in midtown Manhattan, designed by renowned architect I.M. Pei. I quickly became the poster child for successful opening teams—willing to do any job in the food and beverage department with enthusiasm. As a member of this opening team, I saw what it was like to be inspired by leaders. The Four Seasons culture was about taking care of team members and practicing the golden rule of treating others as you wanted to be treated. The standard was excellence in technical skill and in human interaction. It was exciting to be part of that work world.

After the NYC opening, I was tapped to move around the country opening hotels. It meant almost relentless travel, but I still remember opening the Four Seasons in Carlsbad, California, as one of the most fun experiences I ever had. My bosses, Christopher Hunsberger, John O'Sullivan, and Rudi Mack took on the enormous task of opening a gigantic luxury resort while making every day fun. They made the team feel we were part of a mission to deliver something remarkable. They made the work inspiring, which made a lasting impression on me.

Much as I loved the work, it also exacted a price. While I was living in Texas to open the Dallas Four Seasons, I was either working, at home doing laundry and eating tuna sandwiches, or at a bar drinking Shiner Bock beer and playing video trivia. It was intense. On the rare occasions when friends came to visit, they took to calling me "miserable bastard." I was dutiful, responsible, and focused on building a career. The hotel staff served as my only family. I was young and not paying attention to how lopsided my life had become—at least not until I met the woman who would become my wife.

Randi gave me a huge gift by forcing me to look at my work-driven lifestyle. She helped me begin to overcome a kind of social and personal anorexia—I was doing everything for work and very little for anything or anyone else. Trying to change that ingrained behavior helped me recognize how important it is to create a workplace that enables one to have a balanced life. This realization led to what would become a kind of mantra for me: happier at home is happier at work and happier at work is happier at home. It also led to a winding path of study in which Randi and I were partners. Our spiritual explorations prepared us to become parents. It also helped inform the way Erik, Matt, and I came to understand our roles as heart-centered business leaders.

CORE VALUES GUIDE DECISIONS

Culture for me is creating the best version of a close-knit team. Each player owns his or her position with excellence, supports others to win, earns a spot every day by working hard toward a common goal. And yet there's more.

While on a mountain retreat in the early days of Tender Greens, I had a spiritual experience. We were being smudged with sage in the middle of a field when suddenly I was aware of three figures. There was the husband David, the work David, and the spiritual David. Three disparate, nice, well-meaning men. But none of them knew each other—they never talked to one another.

In the moment, I felt they could come together and coalesce in one place. The best of me got to show up at all times. I could be more compassionate at work and more of a leader at home. I could bring all these aspects to my daily life. That was a reckoning for me. I realized I had things to teach at work that were deeper than how to carry plates or ring in orders. I saw that there were aspects of leadership I had compartmentalized that I could bring to my family relationships. I understood that one important aspect of Tender Greens culture was to encourage self-expression for everyone.

There's a quote from Ritz Carlton founder Horst Schulze that for me captures the essence of hospitality: "Elegance without warmth is arrogance." If you can't deliver sincerity, authenticity, and kindness, your "hospitality" rings false. "Elegance" doesn't mean fake formality; from my rebellious days in hotel school, fanciness was something I railed against. At Tender Greens we modeled and encouraged team members to talk to each other and guests as they would to family: respectful and kind but real. They will hear you better and you'll feel better doing it. The more authentic you are, the better.

For most of the Venice, California, high school kids we hired in our initial restaurant, this was their first real job. Coming from tough circumstances, they hadn't yet been taught many constructive life lessons. What Matt, Erik, and I realized fairly quickly was the need for us to be mentors, coaches, and, in some cases, father figures. We'd need to do a certain amount of coaching and butt kicking to get them in line—tough love kind of stuff. But we needed to do more than that.

We were afforded the opportunity to be dads before any of us had kids of our own. That always struck me as an amazing chance to deliver something of value to our young team members. As founders we drew on our collective experience to bring people together around a common goal while teaching them valuable technical and personal skills.

Leadership infused with empathy. Our culture encouraged all team members to work hard, learn stuff, move up, have a good experience. Regardless of whether you come in on the entry level or at a higher position, no matter what you go on to do later in life, we want you to remember your time at Tender Greens as "the best job I ever had."

Our brand was built on the idea of making everyone feel welcome and comfortable. The way a guest feels walking into the restaurant is intrinsically connected to the energy emanating from the people working there. It's not about the color palette, the social media campaign, or the logo. It's about the energy that's being transferred between team members and guests. It's obvious and it's infectious. If somebody feels like this is a happy place, that's the brand experience we wanted to share.

Our goal was to have team members arrive for their Tender Greens shift feeling good to be there. When it doesn't happen, it's a teaching moment for sure. The vibe the staff gives off doesn't lie.

We can all feel the energy in a restaurant right away—and know if it's positive or not. That was an important part of my job—visiting our locations and checking the energy. When it was off, we needed to work with the managers to set things right.

The hard reality is that lots of people in food service work two jobs. They do an AM shift then use their break to get to their PM job. Work hard, sleep for a few hours, do it again. We felt one way we could make working at Tender Greens rewarding was to teach entry-level staff solid skills to enable them to move up. We could be flexible about their schedules so they could make it to their other job or to us. When bad things happened, we needed to be responsive to them—their kid's sick or something went wrong in Mexico and suddenly they had to go back home. Being flexible and compassionate and still getting the restaurant to run isn't ever easy, but it's essential.

Also, what works in one restaurant doesn't automatically carry over as the business expands to more locations. We found over time that while we retained the original elements of our company culture, successful growth sometimes meant emphasizing certain aspects more than others.

In the early days, for example, it felt like we'd created summer camp for chefs—kitchen autonomy without the bureaucracy they'd had to deal with in previous jobs. As the company grew, we needed our chef managers to focus on other things too—the many business necessities for a company to thrive. The culture has to mature without losing the essence of what made it successful. I think this is similar to how I raise my kids—the way I treat my 4-year-old is not the way I treat my 8-year-old. As we mature, we should be able to hear greater truths and take on more responsibility.

At times, this necessary evolution made the culture go off the rails. Periodically conflicts and tensions between the growing home office and the field felt antithetical to what we were trying to be as a company. We were going through growing pains of pushing for margins and developing systems. The restaurants were working really hard to take care of the guests. They didn't want to add more administrative load. Home office staff resented their resistance—as if those people in the field "just don't get it."

As leaders we knew the danger of the home office losing sight of how difficult it is at the restaurant—with staff callouts, equipment malfunctions, orders not showing up, and issues with guests—life in the restaurants is about dealing with the daily wild card. When resentment builds up, separation occurs and it gets really quiet. Communication breaks down. Things get ugly. We spent a lot of time defusing the tensions mostly by urging empathy and understanding from both sides.

When a company moves toward maturity, running the HR department as an administrative compliance tool isn't enough. Just as the main job of the CEO is to grow the company, then someone at that same senior level needs to be watching to make sure the decisions that are being made are reflective of the culture. The growth track is being put through a filter of the company mission, philosophy, and its principles. No matter whether the decision being made is a product change, a service change, or a policy regarding benefits, it must be viewed through the filter of who we strive to be.

Sometimes a decision might be a necessary evil. But we owe it to our team members to explain it as transparently as possible. Don't just drop it on them without showing that it's been thought through and considered from all angles. Be honest in assessing how each decision will impact our team and our guests. We often asked ourselves, "Would we be proud to stand up on stage and announce this?"

EVERYONE MUST ALIGN AROUND CLEAR VALUES

We weren't always perfect at doing so, but mostly you want to hire people who "get it." There were times when we hired the wrong chef or kept the wrong chef too long. But the biggest thing is hiring the right people—those who lead by example, who show it's not just talk, who know that you can succeed with compassion and empathy.

As we took on the next generation of managers, we asked ourselves what we could bring to them. We wanted to develop leaders, chefs and entrepreneurs. For many of our young chefs, it was about recognizing that the old "cheffy" way of doing things—a top down, rule-by-intimidation style—is not a progressive way to inspire people.

We worked to build them as thoughtful servant leaders, engaging their "mom and dad" nurturing qualities at work. I remember sitting with one of our chefs in the Bay Area who was having trouble controlling his anger and frustration. I asked him, "If your kid fell off his bike and badly scraped his knee, how would you react? Similarly, when a team member burns a sheet pan of hazelnuts and you go off the rails, do you believe he woke up thinking 'Today I'm going to go to work and do a really bad job'?" The point was to encourage some charitable assumptions. People generally want to do well but sometimes they mess up.

Pete Balistreri captured our culture best. Whenever I would say I loved something he cooked, he'd always reply, "You can taste the love." And that's absolutely true—genuinely delicious food is made with joy and a loving heart.

Here are some of the keys to developing a culture of leadership and support we tried to instill:

- Listening and working through people's clutter—discriminating between what is being said and what is not being said and reflecting both back to people so they can make better decisions. As the Sufi poet Rumi suggests, "The quieter you become, the more you are able to hear."

- Coaching interpersonal relationships in organizations—using Emotional Intelligence to help leaders grow and work through conflict.

- Helping leaders focus on what's important to them and their businesses—balancing the needs of all stakeholders (team members, investors, suppliers, community) so that everybody wins.

- Helping leaders navigate growth beyond their current comfort zone. Seeing things structurally and being able to create structure where it doesn't exist. Simplifying things that have become overly complicated.

- Establishing organizational leadership competencies for all levels in order to create aligned hiring, training and development practices.

- Providing deep and useful feedback.

- Facilitating holistic strategic planning, mission and principles and business plan elaboration.

- Bringing mindfulness and intentionality into company culture that stands for something and that makes a difference to team members, guests and communities.

- Leaving your ego outside the door and fully supporting your staff to win.

These practices informed our actions and shaped the culture that made Tender Greens a company that talented, good people want to work for.

Chapter 6

Getting Ready to Scale

"If you want to go fast, go alone; if you want to go far, go together"
— *African Proverb*

GET IT RIGHT FROM THE BEGINNING

*B*ecause the three of us came from similar fine-dining pedigrees at places like the Ritz Carlton and Four Seasons, we had each absorbed into our DNA an unwavering commitment to superior guest service. We were used to responding "the answer is yes" to any hospitality request often before we knew the question—and nearly always before we knew how to execute whatever we'd just agreed to. Our Tender Greens principles assumed this level of enlightened hospitality would always be our standard operating procedure.

A shared commitment to consistently delivering an excellent guest experience proved important to shaping Tender Greens in big and small ways. Our culture of authentic hospitality was one of the characteristics that later made us attractive to investment by Danny Meyer, a legendary restaurateur and founder of the Union Square Hospitality Group (USHG).

It's not easy to maintain high service standards even in an expensive fine dining restaurant. But Tender Greens wasn't operating in that rarefied space. We were defining a new level of restaurant experience—an uncharted middle ground between white tablecloth and fast food. From fast food, we were borrowing everyday affordability, speed, and casual convenience. But our food, while approachable, had to be made of the best ingredients skillfully prepared by trained chefs. The service would be authentic, efficient, warm, and inviting. We wanted to create a totally unique dining experience. The more we could succeed at that, the closer we'd come to realizing our ideal—the neighborhood bistro that is reliably welcoming and affordable with nothing cookie cutter about it. And scalable.

Guests were expected to place their order and to carry a tray—a point of much debate for us. How could we solve the ugly tray problem? Eventually, we rejected plastics as "too cafeteria" and went with kitchen-standard aluminum half-sheet trays as more "cheffy." Lining up to place their order and carrying food to their table would be the extent of anything the guest experienced that smacked of fast food. Every interaction with the staff, every service element, every single thing the guests saw, ate, used—the dining room, the bathrooms, the tableware, the non-uniforms of staff—was intended to convey a delightful, elevated-yet-casual dining event. We were implementing the intentions of the business plan at every level of the operation.

Our architect knew we were looking at LEED certification, so he worked with us toward that goal. LEED, which stands for Leadership in Energy and Environmental Design, is a globally recognized green building certification program. Fortunately for us, Bill Terramorse was not a dreamy architect but a very pragmatic one. He convinced us that instead of greenwashing our environmental impact with minor concessions like insulation or an insignificant number of solar panels, we should tackle things that mattered most—lighting choices, energy, and water use.

We wanted Tender Greens to be special and that meant avoiding the commonplace. We were crafting our own playlists—we wouldn't use any music you'd hear on the radio with the possible exception of the local progressive station, KCRW. No Coke or Pepsi products showed up in our beverage selection, no wines you'd be able to buy in the grocery store. No restaurant supplies from Sysco. Tender Greens' supply chain of farmers, artisans, producers, and purveyors had to be transparent and representative of what we stood for. We chose as many local suppliers and service providers as we could. And for the most part, they stayed with us as we grew.

Before it was widely practiced, we were curating the guest experience and our brand identity.

Sometimes our best intentions were missteps. Like those expensive, cool-but-impractical staff aprons that had to be dry cleaned. Or the Tender Greens logo T-shirts we sourced from American Apparel. We went with American Apparel because the shirts were sewn in downtown Los Angeles. We specified our tees had to be made from organic cotton and paid the extra price. When we later discovered that their leadership ethos didn't align with ours, we switched to another supplier.

In visible and invisible ways, we were trying to be mindful of environmental and social concerns—another way we were a bit ahead of the curve. We wanted the Tender Greens brand to demonstrate an authentic commitment to all our values, expressed in many different ways. That became a powerful filter for many decisions.

Just as we were committed to excellent service to our guests, we expected that same service level from our suppliers. From the first day of operations, our volume exceeded our refrigeration capacity. The only way we could maintain quality and freshness was by getting daily deliveries of perishable ingredients like meat. We'd chosen Newport Meat based on our previous relationship with them. When we asked for daily deliveries their answer was "no"; daily deliveries didn't fit their standard of service and it would be inconvenient for them to make an exception for us. After only a week of service, we fired them. Every day, we were working hard to always say "yes" and here was a significant supplier, someone we wanted to grow with us, too quickly and easily saying "no." So we turned to Michael Antoci who would later become our first internal supply chain guy. As we'll see later, we subsequently reconciled with Newport, setting us all up for a long and happy relationship.

Michael's brothers Vito and Tony Antoci owned Superior Anhausner Foods, a local independent quality alternative to a broadline supplier like Sysco. Michael was a sales rep for them. He had been building connections to small ranches with heritage pigs and pastured beef, and he was able to help us out on price and quality. Superior filled the role of a very good meat purveyor for a long time. Eventually we re-hired Newport Meat after they experienced the financial crash in 2008. Seeing how close that brought them to disaster, they'd learned to be far more flexible and customer-centric.

In addition to believing that genuine hospitality meant never saying "no," our training in luxury hotels convinced us of the importance of two golden rules—"treat others as we would like to be treated" and while at work "we are ladies and gentlemen, serving ladies and gentlemen."

Our culture reflects the belief that serving the guest and taking care of each other are equally important. We'd witnessed how this approach is particularly transformative for people from underserved communities who had never experienced anything close to high-level hospitality. We'd seen team members put on a polished persona with their uniform as soon as they came on hotel property. They became somebody different, but not in a phony way. We were going for a more relaxed version of that at Tender Greens. And because it's true that you can't be it if you don't see it, we knew we had to train our team members by modeling our hospitality standards and expectations.

With our decades of service experience, modeling came naturally to us. We'd personally go out of our way without hesitation, just as we'd been taught. We were doing off-menu special orders for guests, wine tastings, and making suggestions for diners.

Our early hires were mostly a bunch of scrappy youths whose main qualifications were strength, stamina, and a willingness to work hard. These weren't culinary school grads who came up through the ranks. Our team members operated in an open kitchen, where every action and reaction was on display and where they were expected to interact with guests. English language skills, not a standard restaurant kitchen requirement, became essential for all team members. Because we had no POS system at the front of the restaurant, the salad maker at the start of the kitchen line had to be fully fluent to take orders and handle guest questions.

We had to train staff to avoid service missteps like the well-intentioned busboy asked by a guest for more salad dressing. We'd schooled him well enough to say, "I'll get that for you" but not well enough to ask, "What kind of dressing do you need?" Asking the cooks for more dressing when we have fourteen varieties only frustrated all parties—cook, busboy, and guest. What we really wanted was for the busboy to be able to identify the salad and ask the kitchen for the right dressing. Until we could bring the entire service staff up to speed, guest interactions with kitchen staff were better experiences than at the table.

DON'T BE TOO PRECIOUS. BE PRACTICAL

When you spend so much time thinking about the details, it's bound to happen that you get really attached to some ideas. Because we were a chef-driven restaurant, a number of these passionately held beliefs were Erik's. His years spent working in some of San Francisco's finest restaurants had deeply influenced him.

One example was Erik's desire to bring the Zuni Café Caesar Salad to Tender Greens. Judy Rodgers's version defined the Caesar in San Francisco, taking a cliché and turning it into a sensation. At Zuni, Caesar salad featured three types of romaine, presented as whole leaves, a "broken" dressing, warm croutons, and parmesan shaved tableside. A beautiful presentation, a bit of dining room flair, and super delicious too. We tried it in those early days with lines out the door. After one disastrous attempt at lunch service, we realized this was an impossibility. We didn't abandon the standard. We designed a better system to deliver on it.

Another hurdle was the emerging concern for food safety and regulations requiring kitchen staff to wear latex gloves. Erik came up in kitchens that taught, depended on, and celebrated hand skills—not just knife work, but scads of jobs done by touch and feel, including the "doneness" or temperature of cooked meats and fish. Ours was not a cuisine created by glove-wearing chefs; it was a system where "tour de main"—exceptional hand skills—were prized and only attained after much practice. Working with that latex membrane between you and your ingredients, you and your tools, was uncomfortable and awkward. However, the optics of the open kitchen, and increasingly regulations, required it. Erik learned to work with gloves as did all the kitchen staff.

Another visual issue was beverages. A tacky brand name beverage cooler was not going to work in our space. We didn't want to display the sodas we carried, even though they were premium brands like Boylan's. Our disappointing early sales indicated unmistakably that if people can't see it, they don't buy it. Once we put the agua fresca out in a bubbler and displayed a few bottles of select sodas, beer, and wine by the cashier, our beverage sales climbed.

To avoid anything too corporate, we dismissed the idea of fully outfitting the staff in uniforms. We provided Tender Greens logo'd T-shirts, hats, and aprons to be worn over their own jeans or chinos. The intent was to give our team members some independence to express their personality in the way they dressed for work. Probably like many school systems and business casual offices, over time we realized not everybody has the taste and style we imagined for them. We found it was better to create some sensible, practical guardrails. This eliminated the need for awkward conversations about inappropriate outfits, hairstyles, or overall appearance.

From an administrative perspective, we were operating small-time—using QuickBooks, staying on top of basics like a team member handbook and required recordkeeping. We were keeping it together and operating legally, fairly, equitably.

Our shareholders and supporters were mostly locals so they were seeing their investment come alive. They were our honored guests, cheering us on from the sidelines. We weren't doing more than sending them a quarterly newsletter, but it was enough to keep them engaged.

Because we had all worked in luxury hotels, we'd been shielded from the food service sectors of takeout, delivery, and drop-off catering. As guests in increasing numbers began to ask for this, we realized we had underestimated the demand. In keeping with our training, we said "yes" even though our small space didn't make this easy. We didn't imagine the volume. By any measure, our first efforts at managing takeout were a mess. The kitchen line wasn't ready for this. Our production system wasn't ready for this. We didn't have enough staff. The physical space wasn't right.

Every inch of the interior had been carefully planned for in-house service. We'd designed a jewelry box that couldn't hold one more earring. Suddenly we had towers of to-go containers and lids in various shapes and sizes and nowhere to store them. Tender Greens had been purpose built, but not for this additional volume.

As more and more people working in neighboring businesses discovered Tender Greens, our takeout and delivery business grew into drop-off office catering. We had additional stress on our taxed little kitchen. We were figuring out how to train delivery drivers, doing drop-offs ourselves, and somehow supervising the dining room. The phone was ringing off the hook. Pages of office orders were pumping out of the fax machine. At times, all three of us might be out on catering deliveries while the restaurant was packed. Our cars were doused in spilled salad dressing, agua fresca, and chicken juice! There were moments when everybody's feet were off the ground. We were all moving at a gallop.

It was impossible to be everywhere at once. We had to build layers of service—and fast. That was Michael Gerber's "E-Myth" advice about early-stage entrepreneurs in action. We had to start taking off management "hats" and, of necessity, setting them on other heads, hoping they could do the job with whatever support we could provide.

Even so, we never felt like the new demands were more than we could handle. The original plan was to grow and we were certainly growing—in volume, reputation, and leadership. We were learning and adapting in real time. Matt was our systems guy to support growth. No matter what the operation was, he was masterful at figuring out how we could improve our processes and standardize our approach. It's one level of challenge to master the production of menu items. But we had much greater challenges to our business model when guest needs and business volume went beyond what we had anticipated.

We were committed to iterate, evolve, try new things. We got out of our preciousness where it was impractical while remaining firmly dedicated to our original intent and value system. It was clear that the time had arrived to build up our bench—to bring in new talent and cultivate talent from within.

BUILD THE TALENT BENCH EARLY

Most of the chefs we worked with dreamed that eventually somebody with money and a passion for their cooking would take them aside and say, "I'd like to back you in your own restaurant."

For the vast majority of chefs, that dream never materializes. Maybe worse is what happens to chefs who get that chance but aren't prepared to be business owners. They think the secret to a successful restaurant is simply excellent food. So not true! And their wealthy backers don't understand the restaurant business, so their advice too often is useless. The partnership goes down in flames fed by hard feelings.

Some chefs make the transition from back of the house to successful entrepreneurs, but usually only when they have industry-savvy partners or deep business experience beyond kitchen management.

From our decades in professional restaurants, we knew lots of chefs who were dreaming of their own place or had been down that road and failed. For chefs who had the talent, discipline, and maturity we wanted in our leaders, Tender Greens was a nearly irresistible offer. Coming into a Tender Greens as executive chef is a nice hybrid—you get to run your own hip, California bistro serving food you're proud of, plus enjoy the prospect of a long-growth runway in terms of broader skills and rewards. Our business plan depended on this.

For us, chef advancement was essentially owner training. We could take a chef who knew how to manage people but who had missed out on financial management, or front of house experience, and provide the training and support to master new skills. Our vision from the beginning was that Tender Greens would always be "chef led," an extremely unusual business model for an industry where power more often resides in "front of house" or guest-facing managers.

To be a truly chef-led organization meant our chefs had to be willing to go "south of the mashed potatoes." They had to leave the comfort zone of the kitchen and work the front of house, interact with guests, manage the numbers, read a financial statement, bus a table, fill in as cashier, even handle equipment troubleshooting and minor maintenance issues. Despite their culinary mastery, they had to accept that they were novices in many other critical aspects of operations.

We'd teach them the entire business. There would be no job in the restaurant they were unable to do well. Once they mastered these skills on the single store level, our growth plan meant future opportunities in regional management with further professional development in compliance issues, leadership, and strategy. All this while staying within one company, not having to job hop or even continent jump to move up. Our proposition was simple: you invest in us and we invest in you, including an equity position—"a fraction of the action."

After our dramatic first-store success, investors wanted to know, "How are you going to scale the three of you?" We already had the answer from many exploratory conversations we'd held with former colleagues. There was a line of great people waiting for their opportunity to join the Tender Greens team.

We were proactively building the bench with chefs, improving our systems as we bumped into inconsistencies and problems. When people asked how we were going to scale production we'd say it's only going to get better—we'll gain valuable experience and insight from each additional chef. Over time, our professional, cross-trained chefs became one of our strongest differentiators.

Besides culinary and leadership talent needs, another important element for growth was our supply chain. We'd been careful in our selection of suppliers who could grow with us. Matt was a key partner in the early development of our supply chain. Having grown up on a farm in Maryland, his appreciation and passion for farming came through on visits to our Southern California partners. With a solid base of suppliers in place, we could grow with confidence. Scarborough Farms, for example, was already committed to supplying thirty future Tender Greens locations. Part of our value proposition to our suppliers was a promise that our business would be great for their business. They signed on in preparation for getting bigger. Thoughtfully building our supply chain proved to be another strong differentiator of our business model.

Without these growth-supporting channels in place for talent and ingredients, getting from one unit to two is nearly like starting over.

We had suppliers we trusted. We recruited leadership depth starting with chefs we'd worked with and knew well. But restaurants need lots of skilled team members to thrive, so next we started to grow internal talent. Purposefully creating a Tender Greens culture of opportunity and support became another key differentiating factor.

Many of our youthful team members lacked more than just professional hospitality training. We taught them dining room etiquette, like how to carry multiple plates and bus glasses without sticking their fingers in them. How to walk through the dining room and see what needs to be done. This was great for operational improvement. But if we wanted them to make progress not just in their jobs but in life, often their needs went beyond technical training.

Unexpectedly, we became family for many of our staff, especially those whose families were absent or broken. Our diverse staff brought cultural differences that showed up in many forms of behavior. Part of our training was lessons about socialization—personal hygiene, controlling or expressing emotion, conflict resolution, personal responsibility and dependability. Developing these life skills became part of our responsibilities as managers and leaders. Seeing young staff transform and grow in their roles was valuable preparation for what would later become our Sustainable Life Project.

LOOK BACK AS YOU MOVE FORWARD

In 2008, after two years in our first store, we looked back. We had immersed ourselves in being bosses and fostering "parents" to our young team members. We were cultivating the next generation of culinary talent. As partners we got better at "training and trusting"—handing over more responsibility to our team to train their members while we continued to train them. We were constantly reminding ourselves to remember what we had already fixed, so as not to make the same mistakes again.

Like everyone who has ever achieved a significant goal, we didn't know how hard it was going to be. We knew how to work long and hard. But when building the business ourselves, there was never any moment when we weren't doing it—no leaving the business behind even if you weren't there. We figured out how to give ourselves some time off, though as owners we were never really "off," we were just not physically in the store. While it was expensive and went on far longer than we had planned, onboarding the chef team of Pete Balistreri and Rian Brandenburg, who would open our second location, helped tremendously—not least because they had cars and could deliver catering orders!

The fact that we didn't anticipate all that was necessary to be the high-volume enterprise we had become was an important learning. We never made that mistake again. In fact, we probably over corrected until we found a better balance.

Something we did well was to remain clear on and true to our standards. We deeply knew the culture we wanted to create—the vision, pathway, and brand we would be proud to own. From day one we followed our plan obsessively while at the same time learning and evolving. Through all the adaptation and revisions, we remained unwaveringly dedicated to our intent and value system. If you don't get it right from the very beginning, you miss your only chance to set the bar and define your standards. It only gets tougher to be great as you get further away from the foundation you built.

The Culver City location taught us a lot and gave us confidence in our plan. Still, when we made the momentous move to a second location, we let emotion cloud our decision-making process. Our San Diego location delivered some new lessons the hard way.

Chapter 7

Early Success is No Guarantee: Recovery Through Innovation

"The Stone Age didn't end because they ran out of stones."
– *Unknown*

*D*espite all the rookie mistakes, our first launch was a home run. Buoyed by confidence that we now knew how to do it, we started to scale with a second location and larger ambitions. Only this time, all our hard-won knowledge didn't buffer us from making a new set of misjudgments. Or being the victim of poor timing.

We opened our second location during the 2008 economic meltdown. We had designed the restaurant based on the lessons of Culver City: bigger, smarter, more room to execute. But then, on opening day, crickets! Now what? In this chapter we'll share what we did to survive and thrive.

EACH RESTAURANT HAS ITS OWN STORY

One risk that every innovator faces is showing the way for imitators. As first movers in fast casual dining, and as pioneers making costly mistakes in designing a new business model, we knew that others would learn from our missteps. We had to get there first.

For instance, our plan identified major California cities that offered Tender Greens the most business opportunity. We had pins in the map all over the state—we especially wanted to be first to market in San Diego, San Francisco, and LA. We knew we'd have to plant the Tender Greens flag in these markets fast if we wanted to build a brand that could create and retain market share in the face of the inevitable copycats that would follow. We started scouting locations in 2007, six months after opening in Culver City, motivated by the urgency to build on the knowledge and momentum we had from the first store.

For our second location early in 2008, we had several major factors in our favor. A proven design template for the store. Solid estimates for time and money to build out the space. A budget enabling us to hire a full-time contractor. We figured a dedicated contractor would save us the anxiety of our first buildout when we'd strung together subs and part-time contracting to save money. On the business side, we had sound operating systems, job descriptions, training protocols, bookkeeping and accounting regimens, extensive menu recipes, and production records. We were primed to repeat our success and demonstrate the portability and scalability of our concept.

Or so we thought.

Chef talent was our most valuable resource. We had been developing a benign form of sleeper cells—chefs in each of the potential locations we were considering who would be ready to join us when we were ready to expand, chefs younger than us suffering from burnout at hotels and fancy restaurants. We knew the ones who were getting crispy but had the culinary chops and the ability to become entrepreneurial. They'd have to forgo some of their creative autonomy but could showcase their talent through menu specials using local foods. In 2007, we activated our first team by bringing Pete Balistreri and Rian Brandenburg from San

Francisco to Culver City to train in preparation for opening our second location.

In keeping with our chef-driven philosophy, Pete was essential to the next location and to the greater Tender Greens story, so this chapter is mostly about him.

When Erik was executive chef at Pan Pacific, Pete was an apprentice. They worked together well, really liked each other, and kept in touch after Erik moved on. Pete was originally from San Diego and had gone to cooking school with Rian. They'd both moved to San Francisco yet shared a desire to move back to their hometown. Pete made the move first, leaving San Francisco to work with Erik and Matt at Shutters on the Beach. Then Pete and Rian signed on with Tender Greens. Pete was with us for nine pre-opening months, longer than we anticipated. That meant commuting back and forth to his young family while we struggled to raise money and assemble the details.

In the spring of 2008, we settled on a location—a former Naval Academy campus, now being tastefully redeveloped as an upscale retail hub. Located about eight minutes outside of downtown San Diego, it was already home to Starbucks, Traders Joe's and similar proven concepts. What's more, Pete and Rian had grown up blocks away and knew everyone. Our site, however, fell far short of meeting the selection criteria we had used so successfully in Culver City.

In Point Loma, we were on the backside of the complex, with no street frontage, practically no signage, and a host of other design and construction issues due to historic landmark restrictions. While there were a few quality businesses already in place, it was still far from a hot retail destination. We questioned the developers about entertainment options and were dismayed that they had no plans for a movie theater. As if these negatives weren't enough to give us pause, it was also a 2½-hour drive from Culver City, hardly a convenient commute for us to oversee a second location.

Pete and his uncle Marc Rose, who was in real estate, were from Point Loma. They felt strongly that this was a special development with a great deal of potential. We had looked at multiple other locations but the obvious markets like La Jolla and San Diego's Gaslamp Quarter were too expensive for us at this stage. To be honest, we let ourselves be charmed by the historic location and the marquee names like Starbucks and Trader Joe's who would be our neighbors.

We had confidence in Pete as a person and as a chef, but we also felt a sense of obligation to him. He had spent more time than expected working with us in Culver City and had made personal sacrifices to stick with us until we could open the second location. Also, Pete and his wife, Giuliana, had invested their retirement savings in Tender Greens. As if that wasn't proof enough of their commitment, they convinced additional Battaglia and Rose family members to invest. The strength of their belief and enthusiasm made it easier to overlook our reservations about the site. We went along with Pete's conviction that it would all work out.

As we knew he would, Pete dug in, taking over the buildout supervision, supplier agreements, and hiring. He believed in Point Loma as perhaps only a native son could. In the summer of 2008, powered by his dedication and talent, we opened our second restaurant.

Our Grand Opening celebration was a lovely party for investors, Pete's and Rian's family, local chefs, and food bloggers to get some buzz going. We made a terrific first impression and many of our guests came back the next day for lunch. But even as lunch was doing OK, dinner business was definitely not happening. Our operating assumptions and financial forecast depended on doing strong headcounts for lunch and dinner. Our playbook was not going to work without serious revision.

INNOVATION IS EVERYONE'S JOB

In the fall of 2008, the U.S. economy began imploding. The development of the Naval Academy campus slowed to a halt. People everywhere were reluctant to spend. We weren't doing any marketing because at the time the only options were print ads, radio spots and couponing which we couldn't afford and didn't believe in. Our biggest challenge became innovating in the moment. How do we keep our product excellent, special, and consistent while also being even scrappier—making the magic happen with fewer resources?

The answers came from Pete. He could have easily gone into victim mode, blamed the failure on us or the economy and made it our problem. Instead, he owned it. This was his store and he was going to rally the team and make it succeed.

Showing his entrepreneurial colors, he didn't want us to turn up in his restaurant with a whole bunch of ideas. He understood what our standards were and he'd figure out how to deliver. He didn't want to give us any excuse to be critical. He wanted it to be right, and Rian was 100% on board. Like true partners, they were not going to let each other down. The challenge made them and their team work really hard.

Our Tender Greens team in Point Loma acquired another important member, Rian's mother, Sue Brandenburg. Rian and Pete had been friends growing up so Sue was already well known to Pete. She joined us as "Pastry Momma" and immediately upped our culinary game. Using local ingredients in their peak seasonal ripeness, Sue's freshly baked tarts, pies, and cobblers won instant guest approval. Paired with her hand-churned ice creams subtly flavored with lavender and other signature additions, Sue's desserts captured the irresistible appeal of the farm stand bakery—homemade deliciousness.

Meanwhile, Pete had to throw much of our operations handbook out the window. We had based our specs on high volume but his restaurant was doing low, erratic volume. Working with suppliers, he was figuring out how to order half-boxes of lettuce and small quantities of perishables to reduce food waste. He revamped production systems and menu items to enable the crew to cook less ahead and do more on demand. He had to accept that sudden bursts in business would mean 86ing some items. His focus was to reduce cost and waste while maintaining excellent quality.

Managing products is one challenge; managing people is even trickier. We couldn't afford staffing comparable to our Culver City level. Pete broke apart our ironclad job descriptions and introduced cross-training—the cashier could do more things, the busser could make agua fresca, and so on. He devised a more flexible and fluid set of roles, doing more with fewer people—managing down the labor costs while keeping service standards high. His approach proved to be a valuable contribution to all Tender Greens operations.

As any businessperson will tell you, you can't save your way to prosperity. Driving revenue has got to happen. On this front too, Pete got super creative. He invested time outside the restaurant to serve as brand ambassador for Tender Greens. Pete participated in fine dining chef events all over San Diego to get our name out.

He had serious culinary chops, so no one was dismissing him by saying "Go back to your salad joint." Pete was buying heritage pigs, breaking them down, making salumi; getting fresh fish off the docks and making crudo; picking fresh produce from neighboring Point Loma Farms in the morning for lunch specials that day—all ingredients that food enthusiasts couldn't get elsewhere at close to Tender Green's prices. Pete was determined to bring people in the door whatever it took. He used his hometown connections and the press began to play up the "native son returns home" angle.

Buzz started to build as Tender Greens became known as the place chefs would go to eat on their day off. From there, the word reached foodies who were economizing, but also a broad demographic of people who discovered how approachable and affordable we were. Retirees, couples on first dates, construction workers, folks from the nearby church and schools. The value proposition of Tender Greens started to take hold in the San Diego culture of healthy eating.

Pete drove innovation primarily from the kitchen. But the staff he hired also contributed to our evolution. At our first store, we focused more on a worker's abilities and attitudes than on their aesthetics. The Point Loma staff drew our attention to their appearance. Reflective of the culture of health and wellness prevalent in San Diego, this was already an attractive crew. Disappointed by our unisex approach to uniform apparel, the women advocated for V-neck instead of crew neck tees; for yoga pants, not cargo pants; headbands instead of hats. As a result, everybody looked great and felt great. We would not have gotten to that without listening to our staff. Pete gets credit for this too. His hiring practice was to find one good team member, then encourage them to get their friends to apply. In this way, he built high-quality hospitality and close-knit teams from within.

MAKE IT EASY FOR YOUR PEOPLE TO DO GREAT

In hindsight, opening a second location 2½ hours away didn't make for timely management. We worked out a plan where one or two of us partners would go down once a week to give Pete and Rian a night off. Ever frugal, we stayed at a motel so dingy that David wouldn't take his socks off. We'd run a full day shift on our own, then debrief Pete and Rian about things they needed to work on. We'd try to keep this high level, supported by specific observations.

The hospitality business is a gigantic bunch of details, viewed from multiple perspectives—what the chef sees, what the floor staff sees, and ultimately what the guest sees. Developing that 360-degree view is crucial to creating a great guest experience and a profitable business.

If, for example, the floor staff fills a squeeze bottle with dressing without shaking the larger dressing container, the squeeze bottle is all oil. Chefs know that but staff may not. The chef manager had to make sure all eyes were on all potential problem areas—is the ice machine clean, are the table legs being leveled with sugar packets, are the bathrooms immaculate and well-stocked, the lighting level and music volume just right? These were the things we had to institutionalize to make sure the brand was consistent.

Our San Diego team nicknamed David "Mr. Wolf" from the movie *Pulp Fiction*. He earned the name by being the pickiest of us about dining room operations. He'd walk the floor with the manager and find thirty things that needed fixing. The object was not to humiliate or torment; it was to develop the same ability David has to see the details. After one of these walks, the manager would correct the deficiencies. From then on all those items will be part of his or her vision. Our managing chefs had to teach their floor crew to really *see* the dining room, just as they taught the cooks to taste and adjust the mashed potatoes and soup before every service.

Part of Pete's maturation as an entrepreneur was to recognize that everything he did impacted the brand. As a chef, he would never compromise culinary quality, but it seemed acceptable to make cuts in other areas. For instance, he thought the flatware we chose for Tender Greens was too expensive. Without asking, he bought a cheap alternative at Restaurant Depot that looked like Denny's flatware. We pushed back on that. We wanted to be profitable, but not in ways that negatively impact our guests. He bought the good silverware.

These are practical details, but we also charged Pete with "owner-level" details of financial management. We'd review the financial indicators on a weekly basis and ask him, "How do we fix this issue?" We were developing his financial chops by sharing the P&L and general ledger. The chef checked for correctness but would also see the impact of unnecessary overtime and waste. This became standard practice for us as we grew. With each of our chef leaders, we were 100% transparent about how the overall business was doing, how each unit was performing, and how they compared to the other Tender Greens units.

Even when San Diego was underperforming, it was a beautiful space, almost always perfect when we walked in. The food was exceptional. Pete was fully aware of the problems and was eager to fix them. He made us get off our high horse about leftovers, which we had sworn we would never carry over to next day service. Pete helped us see that we could use leftover steak to make delicious chili. He showed us how to repurpose over-produced items into stews, soups and other dishes that improve with time. His commitment to reducing food costs morphed into much smarter, better food utilization for us as a company. Without a doubt, Pete's Point Loma innovations, when replicated in Culver City, made our flagship restaurant more profitable.

In the early months, we partners were joined at the hip with Pete and Rian, but we also had this very busy restaurant in Culver City. We'd go down to San Diego, then too often return to Culver City only to find conditions less than ideal—dining room lights on full blast or in that weird dim-and-grim transition; music blaring on the wrong playlist or turned off because the playlist had ended; no candles on the tables; cashier area a mess; a busser out front leaning on the wall watching people go by.

Our absences enabled us to see which staff we could count on and who just talked a good game. Hourly team members like Lacy Moody were invaluable. When Lacy applied for a job, her resume was sparse—sandwich maker at Quiznos summed up her restaurant experience. However, something about her earnestness, her seriousness, and her smile made us hire her.

From day one, Lacy was focused and in the zone. Quiet but eyes wide open—watching and absorbing. Every plate she made was done to standard: perfect portioning, perfect seasoning, perfect presentation. She was fast too. Over time, we taught her how to braise, grill, carve, and cashier. With each new challenge, Lacy quietly delivered.

We saw the need to elevate relatively inexperienced team members with potential to roles as team leaders. When we asked Lacy to run a shift so we could stop experiencing the evening change-over failures, she came through. We'd come back from San Diego to find our little restaurant humming. Lacy rose through the Tender Greens ranks and became a respected executive chef.

Advancing great team members has been one of our greatest joys and, with Lacy and other stellar team members stepping into leadership roles, it meant we could turn our attention to Job No. 1—creating more restaurants people really love.

BE PATIENT

The slow start in San Diego meant that to some extent Culver City was still bankrolling it. Point Loma was the first location that wasn't "founder-led." Rather than taking it over, we intentionally gave the leadership team the goal of getting in the black. We had the opportunity to see right away that by empowering them to figure it out, the right leaders could and would be successful. Because of Pete's many pivots, he eventually achieved profitability, despite the challenge of disappointing initial volume.

That was a validating lesson for us—to trust that improvement does not have to come exclusively from the owners. If we chose the right leaders, we could allow them to innovate. Our role was to share the vision for Tender Greens. Leaders like Pete Balistreri like to be told what the end game is, but not how to get there, and certainly not how to do their jobs.

Still this slow start was a setback. We thought we'd generate more cash and be able to open the next one or two units sooner. Instead, we were back out with our dog-and-pony show seeking investors. As it turned out, the first ten years was pretty much perpetual fundraising to get out from under the need for capital. Even though this demanded much of our time, we believe this approach enabled us to retain more control over our growth rate and preserve equity for our shareholders and for us.

For sure, there were times when we wished we could take all the money we put into San Diego and move it somewhere else. We had a ten-year lease with two five-year renewal options. We had to ride it out. This lease length became our standard. We were always in it for the distance. We did not want to find ourselves in that vulnerable place where a restaurant succeeds only to see its rent unsustainably jacked up at the end of the first five-year term. We wanted to have options if a location was riding high and still in great shape. And we wanted the time to build to that performance level.

Eventually the San Diego location caught on. It was performing profitably and made for a terrific story—two local boys, boasting culinary chops that people found amazing. Even more success lay ahead for Pete, Rian, and the Point Loma team.

Part of Pete's motivation was his belief that his hometown was always eclipsed by the flashier restaurant scenes in LA and San Francisco. He wanted to prove that San Diego deserved culinary respect and attention. He applied his considerable talent and his Italian American roots to the locally sourced ingredients he sought out. His talent and knowledge made him a magnet for young cooks in the area. Working with him enabled aspiring chefs to learn deeper culinary skills like whole-animal utilization and the complex, nearly lost arts of charcuterie and salumi. Pete's passion for culinary excellence rippled out. His success at Tender Greens showed us that developing homegrown talent can pay unanticipated dividends.

One more important thing happened in San Diego that had profound implications for Tender Greens. Pete held on to the discipline, commitment to teamwork, and deference to the coach he learned from playing football in high school and college. His culinary experience in high-profile kitchens came at a time when "Rule No. 1 was: The chef is always right. Rule No. 2 is: If the chef is ever wrong, see Rule No. 1." Once he was in charge, he came to see that being the chef as the unquestioned leader is integral to getting the job done in the moment. However, he also started to recognize his deeper responsibility as a nurturing leader and quasi-parent to his young staff. Over time, he learned to soften his delivery, to get his point across without being fiery. His mantra echoed that of the legendary horse trainer, Buck Brannaman. "Be gentle in what you do, firm in how you do it."

For the lasting benefit of our early stage chef-driven business, Pete recognized that the infallible, omnipotent chef leader thing was outdated. It was not the best way to get good people to respond well. By radically altering his leadership style, Pete Balistreri became the greatest incubator of talent in our company.

Years later, we instituted the "Golden Goat" award, a ridiculous oversized trophy with a goat on top that was earned quarterly by our most successful restaurants. It was a big deal and a source of pride. Along with the trophy, the winning managers won dinner with the three founders at a restaurant of the winner's choice. When Pete and Rian won, we enjoyed a great, somewhat boozy dinner at Juniper & Ivy in San Diego's Little Italy. They got a little chatty, relaxing enough to kind of forget we were the "bosses." Out came details from a few early stories we'd never heard before.

Nothing illegal or immoral, but Pete and Rian had found some creative ways to establish standards and discipline that were decidedly *not* part of the Tender Greens handbook. Some were funny, others somewhat cringeworthy. If a team member had been goofing off or letting the team down, the chef sent the offender into the walk-in refrigerator to count fennel bulbs. They'd emerge, chilled and chastened, to report, "Chef, there are 23 fennel bulbs in the walk-in." The chef would send them back in to do a recount, "Just to be sure." No real harm done, but an example made to the entire team.

Some of their stories poked fun at themselves, as well, prompting belly laughs 'til we had tears rolling down our faces. In the end, they succeeded in putting Tender Greens on the map in San Diego. We were pleased with the success of our second restaurant, but especially proud of Pete, Rian, and their team.

Next up in 2009 was West Hollywood where we built a splashy, big footprint store. This was in the heart of a proud gay neighborhood and it was obvious from the start that we were a hetero company. To acknowledge and respect the uniqueness of the neighborhood, we'd commissioned gigantic reproductions of

Hank O'Neal's historic photos of early gay pride parades in New York's Greenwich Village. The prints weren't ready by opening day so we scrapped our big opening plans and did a soft opening, nothing more than bunches of helium balloons brought in daily by one of our investors. People were trickling in, drawn by the gorgeous food, but it was quiet.

When the artwork was ready, we held our grand opening as a fundraiser for the Los Angeles Gay and Lesbian Center (now the Los Angeles LGBT Center). It was worth the wait. The restaurant became the go-to café for the city of West Hollywood. A measure of patience while we waited for the defining artwork made all the difference. And it sure felt great to bounce back after San Diego and the recession. This was the beginning of Tender Greens' rapid expansion, fueled in part by the market opportunities the 2008 downturn had created.

Chapter 8

When a Downside Has an Upside

"Option A is not available. So let's kick the sh** out of option B."
—Sheryl Sandberg

B*usiness school students learn to consider the "macro" or exter-*
nal forces that no one can control, like recessions or natural disasters
or radical changes in cultural norms. Even so, every such event may
be a threat to some businesses but an opportunity for others. Ask
any entrepreneur who lived through the market crash of 2008 or
the 2020 pandemic and they'll tell you they learned some powerful
lessons about agility.

We came out of the 2008 economic downturn well ahead of the pack,
with stellar real estate, stronger systems, an organizational road-
map, best-in-class talent, and a culture of patience for long-term
goal achievement. In this chapter, we discuss what we overcame that
helped us thrive when others were struggling.

GROW TOGETHER, NOT APART

What we remember most clearly about this time from 2009-2011
is being very, very busy. We started to divide our roles as partners,
deepen our individual expertise, and conquer new challenges

as they kept coming. To support the growth trajectory we were on, we each started running in separate directions based on our strengths and interests.

In the early days Matt was our handyman who fixed anything we couldn't afford to have done professionally. Over the years his skills evolved as he taught himself Google Sketch Up and CAD. Matt dug into real estate and facilities issues, forging relationships with architects, contractors, and facilities management companies—all while scouting new locations. At 6' 4" with a classic boyish handsomeness that nearly landed him a spot on *The Bachelor (Season 3)*, Matt's presence on a construction site was key. He led with respect for the trades, credibility based on his knowledge, and the strength to push back when things started to go off course. He deserves much of the credit for the design, functionality, and unique character of our restaurants.

David ran the flagship Culver City restaurant as our home office "base camp" while identifying banks, attorneys, accountants, and others who could address our many increasingly complex business needs.

Erik took to the road, regularly visiting all Tender Greens locations, coaching the operations teams, establishing our supply chain in new regions, and taking the lead representing the brand through marketing events and social media.

This early expansion phase gave each of us space to develop our next level of executive knowledge. It was an exciting time but it also created some isolation. Separated physically and absorbed in different aspects of our explosively growing business, we often felt the pains of disconnection. We were getting siloed. Each of us pursued what we believed were the most burning issues for the company. We had a sense of opportunity and urgency, and we were all working full tilt. What we lacked was a dependable feedback loop.

David describes what happened to our partnership structure as "moving from a totally sturdy three-legged stool to three wobbly one-legged stools, to three pogo sticks going in all directions."

Individually and collectively, we had reached the end of the runway of our professional experience. None of us had managed multi-units in different cities. We hadn't built enough relationships with people who understood scale. Too much of our energy was going into figuring things out. Now we had four restaurants that required organization-building activities. It was very much learning on the job as growth pushed us way beyond things we'd done in any of our previous management roles.

It can be hard to report back to your partners when you're busy figuring it out. We were each working to build expertise that would give us the confidence to bring our actions and decisions to the partnership. But we were getting locked into our own stuff, quietly suffering until complaints about each other began to surface. Most importantly, we were not using each other for support as we should have.

Before we went too far into isolation, we thought back to the partnership pledges we made at the start. We saw that when we went quiet for too long, misunderstandings increased. Scheduled meetings were productive, but we were missing the micro-collaborations so typical of our early days—the quick "What's up?" and "How's your day?" calls. We had to regroup and realign. We needed a new way to stay in close touch.

BE GUIDED BY GREATER EXPERIENCE FROM TRUSTED SOURCES

Around this time we met Frank Vizcarra who proved to be a major force for good in our future. Frank was a former McDonald's executive who discovered Tender Greens as a guest at the Point Loma restaurant. From his successful career with McDonald's, Frank was keenly attuned to industry innovation, especially in the quick serve sector. He immediately saw that we were on to something. His initial approach to us was an offer to invest. But after David met with him, Frank's industry knowledge, wide network, and expertise offered even more value than his cash.

You might be wondering, what could be worse than to fall under the influence of someone from the global fast food industry? We were a bit skeptical at first. We were so tied to the ideal of being "special" that anything resembling corporate practices seemed threatening to our identity. Frank persistently showed us otherwise.

His level-headed approach to problem solving and conflict resolution was part of Frank's initial appeal. We had so much on our plates. Beyond our 2/3 majority vote, there was no structured methodology for making smart, data-based decisions. We had to create our own new cadence and we needed help doing that.

Things bubbled up when the three of us were meeting in Frank's kitchen. We reached a stalemate about investing in training team members on equipment. One opinion was that staff were always breaking the equipment, so we should limit who is allowed to use certain pieces. A counter opinion was that if we didn't train more staff on safe equipment use, we were limiting our productivity as well as holding staff back from advancement. That was only the tip of the disagreement.

A deeper issue was not having a reliable system in place to deal with broken equipment. Should we maintain replacement parts and extra equipment at each site? What protocols were in place for repairs? The conflict wasn't limited to who was breaking what equipment. The larger issue was living up to our commitment to create systems that made it possible for our team members to do great work. If they were falling short of that, either the system was broken or the person was not a good fit.

Our 2/3 ratification process couldn't work for decisions like these that affected the whole company. If we all weren't 100% convinced, we'd be missing a third of the energy needed to implement a practice throughout the organization. It became apparent that if all of us did not support a direction, this issue and others like it would be doomed to fail. It wasn't so much consensus we were after as it was a unanimous commitment to support change.

A fundamental resistance to systemization often came down to finding balance between our desire to foster innovation and our need for simpler solutions to persistent problems. In some instances, we were convinced that designing systems to standardize many of our operations would ensure greater efficiency, consistency, and profitability. Seemingly simple but often neglected things like providing each restaurant manager with a lightbulb spec sheet for the designer lighting fixtures, along with inventory pars, sources to purchase replacements, and a ladder to reach the lights. Without a complete system in place, our managers were as frustrated as we were by not being able to replace burnt-out bulbs. Other efforts at systematizing, especially those that involved our menus, raised concerns that imposing rigid systems would kill the creative drive of our chefs.

Frank's world of systems expertise, honed at McDonald's, ran counter to Erik's determination to hold on to the Tender Greens idea of a chef-centric model. He did not want to sacrifice this core value and put us on a path to merely imitating other models like California Pizza Kitchen. The gravity of a meeting exploring kitchen standardization, Erik recalls, was "shocking enough to my system that I left it determined to give myself a week to marinate. I had a trust gap with Frank that needed to be acknowledged and resolved."

Part of our growing pains as a company and as leaders meant honestly re-evaluating our positions—being honest about our biases, listening to other voices. By his calm and patient approach, Frank helped us find our way past what could sometimes be a stubborn insistence on independence as the best way to protect creativity. Without doubt, his encouragement for Tender Greens to design better, purpose-built systems that fit who we were moved us forward as a company and as leaders.

Geographic expansion meant investing a great deal of time in identifying and nurturing many critical new relationships—not only with investors, advisors, service providers, local governments, and community groups, but also with guests. We were proactive about digging into our communities, joining relevant boards like the Hollywood Farmers Market or Culver City Downtown Business Association, and making a meaningful contribution to neighborhoods where we did business. We were also on the lookout for external partners from those groups who over time would become trusted members of our Tender Greens family. Frank Vizcarra proved to be one of these.

MOMENTUM MATTERS

Despite the recession, our Culver City restaurant revenues continued to come in 300% over the original budget. We were feeling confident that Tender Greens had tapped into a real need in the marketplace—delicious food at an affordable price in a comfortable, welcoming setting.

In pitch meetings, we'd see how impressed potential investors were when we shared the extraordinary store-level economics Tender Greens posted during a recession. In retrospect, it was astonishing. But being mostly head down on the line in those days, we didn't think much about the recession in Culver City.

We had different street-level views in San Diego and in Hollywood. We'd scan the nearly empty Naval Academy campus in Point Loma, dismayed by the still-empty spaces meant for Crate & Barrel, Barnes & Noble, and others. At Hollywood's Sunset & Vine, the Wells Fargo bank was shuttered, Borders Books was closed, all sorts of businesses had gone Chapter 11. The lights in Hollywood had gone a bit dark. We would walk the neighborhood at night and wonder "What happened here?"

As it dragged on, the recession and its effects were causing us to look at new angles for our existing restaurants. That put us on the creative offense—we introduced a Sunday beer garden, for example, to build more traffic. We also got more active on social media. We took nothing for granted.

Like any expanding business, we needed affordable leases, talented team members, and new infusions of capital. Fortunately, the recession helped us access real estate and people. With so many businesses downsizing or failing outright, we were able to attract great people, from chefs to cashiers. Many of these hires would later become restaurant- and company-level leaders.

Government-backed loans helped with capital.

Just as importantly, the company was solvent with a growing bank account. We were scrappy, frugal, and constantly evaluating every expense. We were determined to build reserves so we'd have some financial security. Reserves would help us weather business disruptions like earthquakes, fires, construction delays—any number of things beyond our control—and buy some peace of mind against the unforeseen.

Our original capital plan had not been realistic—how much we would need, how long it would last, the company's ability to contribute to growth. Everything took longer than we projected, especially store openings. We were signing leases faster than the money to build them out could come in. As a consequence, we were always looking for additional capital beyond what the business could self-finance. We'd been successful working our existing relationships, but for the next round of growth we would need to look elsewhere.

As founders we were protective of our equity stake. Every time we went out for money it was a dilution of our equity. As noted previously, we started to take meetings with private equity to explore that world and possibly get some free consulting from their analysis of our business. Ultimately, we pressed the pause button on equity rounds and instead financed our next wave of growth by securing consecutive SBA loans whose low-cost millions helped keep us on track.

We learned that the time spent making sound real estate decisions was worth it. We wanted to get to thirty stores, but we needed to make sure that each real estate decision would be the right one long-term.

After a slower than hoped but still remarkable start, we were catching up to our growth plan. With successful openings in West Hollywood and Hollywood, we had a lot of wind in our sails. In quick succession, we opened in key neighborhoods—Walnut Creek in the San Francisco Bay Area, Pasadena and Santa Monica in Southern California. This last group in 2013-14 marked a really big leap for us.

As we grew, systems that honored our values were becoming ever more important to provide consistency. We were adopting and refining some of our mentor Frank Vizcarra's suggestions derived from his McDonald's experience. One stellar example was the work we asked Fermin Arias, our LA regional chef, to undertake. His task was to develop a best practices "book" that would come to define our standard operating procedures (SOPs) and serve as a training and station guide. Fermin did the slow, hard work of building this book with input from all our chefs. Their collective experience and insights led to documenting the most effective ways to achieve consistent high-quality culinary production—line checks, detailed descriptions of each station, and countless other important details created and vetted by our chefs. The work took him over a year but became a major resource for our company.

With this cluster of new restaurants around the state, we partners began to take what we had learned individually and build our own departments around our expertise: business and operations management; site selection and development; culinary excellence and supply chain. By benefiting from expertise beyond our own, we had moved Tender Greens to a new level of professionalism. Reaching this stage of maturity for the business and for our partnership created the space to deepen the expressions of our values.

From its inception, Tender Greens aimed to generate positive social impact. In our early days, we focused on building an equitable supply chain, serving healthy and wholesome food, and creating a workplace culture that was accepting, respectful, nurturing, and often even fun. Once we had this foundation in place and had confidence in the financial health of the business, we were able to invest more meaningfully in our communities. The time was right for the Sustainable Life Project to be born.

Chapter 9

Mission at the Core: The Sustainable Life Project

"Most of the important things in the world have been accomplished by people who have kept on trying when there seemed to be no hope at all."
– *Dale Carnegie*

T his chapter is Erik's origin story, which we include to delve into what motivated him as a person and as a restaurant professional.

Whatever business you've built, your first obligation is to ensure the viability and resilience of your enterprise. That means profit for starters. Predictably stable sources of revenue, a committed and talented workforce, sound partnerships with suppliers, and confidence in the future all have to be in place before you can seriously consider creating a new business line for external social impact.

The drive for profit should never preclude your business from embodying your core values, even from its inception. A humane company culture, fair wages and employment practices, equitable relationships with suppliers, respectful guest relations, environmentally responsible operations—all of this can and should be part of the DNA of your business. Going one step further, these features should be in place before trying to extend the scope of "good works" if you want to have your efforts respected as authentic and not easily dismissed as greenwashing.

The success of Tender Greens showed there was a huge appetite for the foods we loved and wanted to share; meeting that need filled a professional goal for me. But it also allowed a personal goal to surface, a commitment I made only to myself decades earlier, a pledge to make a difference beyond cooking.

In 1986, I left my hometown of Kutztown, Pennsylvania, to start college at Temple University in North Philadelphia. Kutztown, whose tagline is "A most agreeable town," is a rural college town less than seventy-five miles from Philly. Nothing in my small town background prepared me for Philly's tough streets. The hollowed-out neighborhoods, rampant crime, and chronic homelessness were a constant reminder of failed policies.

New York City and other aging cities like Philadelphia had fallen into urban decay. The flight of businesses and residents to the suburbs, the exodus of young people in search of more opportunity, the gutting of the tax base all contributed to a pervasive spirit of multi-generational despair among those left behind. Philadelphia, the "City of Brotherly Love," had long grown away from its founding identity into one of underachieving aggression.

The view from my freshman dorm room was of two cities. The towering new skyscrapers of Center City symbolized the unlimited potential ahead; the gritty blocks surrounding Temple's campus told a story of hopelessness. I made a promise to myself that if my future proved profitable, I would someday return to help those left behind.

After college I went to culinary school in Providence, Rhode Island, before escaping the cold weather for California. My years cooking in San Francisco left little room or resources to look beyond my own career and self-interest. As a chef, I would participate in the big fundraisers dotted with celebrities in hopes of photo ops with my more famous colleagues. We would try to outdo each other creatively while rarely thinking about the charitable work the event funded. It always felt a bit fake and empty to me.

I remember reading an article about celebrity chef Jeremiah Tower of Stars, at the height of his career, criticizing the charity industry. He was shown on the cover of the *San Francisco Chronicle* in chef's whites, pockets turned out with a few coins falling to the ground around him. The story depicted what amounted to a shakedown of prominent restaurants, death by endless $25 donations. Every charity had its hand out. Someone was at your door every day, guilting you into meaningless giving that wasn't likely to matter, yet amounted to thousands of donated dollars from your meager budget. These organizations were no doubt trying to do good work, but the lack of accountability coupled with the absence of connection to donors contributed to growing resentment, especially in the low-margin but high-profile restaurant industry.

Part of our founding intentions at Tender Greens was to give back in meaningful ways. By the time we had four restaurants, I asked all our chefs to get involved in something that mattered to them. They went for all sorts of things—animal rights, educational programs, environmental issues. I was living just a few blocks off Venice Beach. Like many progressive California neighborhoods, Venice was a target destination for wayward youth. Old emotions around homelessness surfaced. I channeled my community efforts into finding ways to make a difference in young people's lives.

START SMALL. FIGURE IT OUT

I'm serious when I say that starting a social impact initiative requires at least as much due diligence as you invested in vetting
your initial business idea, or any new line of products or services.
A short checklist of steps and questions:

- Do the research and ask around.
- Start with the need—not yours but the community's.
- Be realistic about the resources and skills your organiza-
  tion brings to the solution.
- Are you trespassing on the turf of established and impact-
  ful nonprofits?
- Where is the intersection between an unmet need and
  your capabilities?

I was introduced to Judy Runan, the executive director of Stand
Up for Kids, a nonprofit centered on emancipated foster youth.
These street kids have nothing. No family to speak of. No security
net to fall back on. Left to fend for themselves until caught in the
sinkhole of drugs, prison, prostitution, or death. Little hope for
any meaningful future, much less a bright one.

I had mostly written them off myself after decades of stepping
over them in Venice, Hollywood, and the Lower Haight in San
Francisco. Then something changed for me. I started to listen.
First, to the executive director of Stand Up for Kids and then
to the kids themselves. Each had a unique story, the next more
alarming than the previous. The through line was foster care. I
believed Tender Greens could catch them before they fell through
the cracks. We could offer a path forward toward independence.

I wanted to do something that got to the root and changed the
course they were on. The kids were food insecure. We had good

food in abundance. They lacked skills to navigate a competitive city. We had talented chefs who could mentor them. They had been let down by a system ill-equipped to absorb them. We were building a workplace culture grounded in small-town values and welcoming to people of diverse backgrounds. For many young people who had never quite fit in, we provided a place of belonging.

We started by selecting those kids most likely to succeed. One by one, we got them in training with willing members of our team. Our basic curriculum had three elements of foundational life skills:

- *Where does food come from?* We organized visits with farmers and makers.
- *How do you cook?* We offered culinary instruction from food safety to advanced pastry.
- *How do you work?* We provided apprenticeship and mentoring in a Tender Greens restaurant.

We had lots of attrition in the beginning. Mental health issues, legal troubles, the intensity of a restaurant—all competed with our desire to nurture these kids. Eventually, despite our best efforts and intentions, all the participants failed to find long-term independence. We pressed pause to rethink the program.

What we learned from the pilot became the basis of a thorough redesign. The youth we decided to invest in were aging out of the foster care system or "emancipated foster youth." Statistically, this group is the most likely to fall through the cracks of society. Around age 18, after maybe a decade or more of foster care, they were given a backpack and $200 and sent on their way. Not exactly a recipe for success. My preference would have been to catch kids even earlier. But younger kids raise complications, with legal restrictions preventing them from integrating fully into the workplace.

Some organizations were doing good work with young adults, but it seemed no one had found all the answers. By homing in on that group, we were filling a need that otherwise would go unmet.

One of the critical needs for these kids is money, so we shifted to paid internships. Instead of exposing them to high-minded concepts like artisan growers and refined culinary techniques, we focused on developing competence in repetitive tasks and fundamental skills. If they mastered these by the time they completed the program, they were job ready for a paid position in the dishwashing or food prep stations of a kitchen, where most new team members start. For life skills, they learned about access to better food, what it means to come to work on time, groomed and ready to go, how to integrate into a work team, and possibly even how to find a career path forward. We wanted them to be successful team members, if not for Tender Greens, then for some other enterprise.

I like to think big, but building a small model to learn from proved to be a more reliable path to accomplishment. Testing a prototype meant we could fail small without losing sight of my bigger aspirations. If we could accept that achieving a big vision meant taking a patient approach, it was easier to get started. A cutting board, a knife, a case of salad greens, and one kid can add up to mentorship. That was a revelation for us.

We had to set expectations and accountabilities as part of the necessary life skills we wanted to impart to our trainees. Setting clear expectations also helped to buffer us from burnout. As a company we set limits on the resources—time, money, and talent—that we were willing and able to commit to our impact initiative. We made ourselves clearly identify what success would look like and acknowledge which outcomes would indicate failure. These questions are not as simple as they may sound. But addressing them kept us honest and made us more resourceful.

FIND THE RIGHT PARTNERS

At this time, we considered forming a 501(c)3 as a nonprofit arm to Tender Greens. We decided against that route because it felt too restrictive. We did not want to spend any time on fundraising and we believed with careful planning we had the capacity to self-finance. We wanted to set and measure our own benchmarks of success. This decision, in combination with some key hires and organizational restructuring, led to the professionalization of what became well-established as the Sustainable Life Project (SLP). This project quickly helped shape the culture of Tender Greens, enhanced our identity as a community-based business, and distinguished us as an employer of choice.

Stand Up for Kids was our introduction to powerful partnerships. By working with this organization, we were able to benefit from its deep experience. It opened our eyes to the tremendous potential for the multiplier effect of collaboration with well-chosen partners. It inspired Tender Greens to find ways to be additive in all future partnerships and collaborations and to avoid the common trap of trying to go it alone.

So many entrepreneurs self-protect, toiling away in the silo of their own creation, reluctant to foster or connect with a supportive network. This is worse than leaving money on the table. No matter what an organization does, there's an ecosystem surrounding it. For restaurants, that ecosystem includes farmers, makers, artisan producers—all sorts of individuals and businesses that exist outside of an organization but can meaningfully contribute to its success if invited to do so. Our experience has repeatedly shown that the best outcomes are never the work of an individual or even of a single business.

We worked closely with diverse nonprofit organizations including Participant Media, Inner City Arts, Homeboy Industries, LA

Kitchen, and Covenant House in our journey to find the right template for the Sustainable Life Project. Like every for-profit entity, these nonprofits had finite resources of money, time, expertise, and facilities. All too often they had to compete against each other for donors and grants, just as for-profit companies view other businesses as competition for guests.

The decision by Tender Greens to self-fund rather than forming a 501(c)3 meant that we wouldn't be competing for or distracted by fund raising.. This enabled us to move freely in the nonprofit sector, looking for relationships that could be value-added for both parties. We started scouting for a fit between our limits and their limits, and for mission alignment. Collaboration around common goals with a crystal-clear understanding of pooling resources—rather than competing for them—ensures scaling of impact, every time.

One of our most important partnerships was with Covenant House in Hollywood. It was well resourced with great programming for mental health, housing, financial guidance, and work placement for youth experiencing homelessness, abuse, and trafficking. Covenant had a strong track record of preparing kids for work but lacked the connections to open employment doors. This is where Tender Greens could offer true partnership. Covenant House took care of those early stage needs we were ill-equipped to manage, and we enabled paths forward by providing jobs in food and hospitality.

Inner City Arts, another amazing partner in downtown Los Angeles, always wanted a culinary program. It was very well networked; they introduced us to many powerful, effective change agents within the Los Angeles impact community. Inner City Arts created opportunities for Tender Greens to add what we had to offer, beginning with a culinary program. Eventually this relationship led to a meaningful personal and professional commitment when I became a founding board member of LA Kitchen, started by Robert Eggers.

The most enduring partners were the people who saw Tender Greens as adding something their organization wanted and lacked. Our responsibility was to make sure the partner organizations brought what we needed. Success depends on collaboration without restrictions or competition—we can't be fighting for the same market share or donor base. Our partnership agreements enabled us to operate freely, with frank agreement on financing, mission, and scope of work. Committing Tender Greens as a self-funded, for-profit business enabled us to navigate in the nonprofit sector without posing a threat to others. We pledged our own resources and would never go after their donor base or grant funders.

MAKE IMPACT FUNDAMENTAL TO YOUR BUSINESS

Even with the strength of our new connections in the mission-driven community, our Sustainable Life Project took time to establish. Employee buy-in didn't happen right away. It took some proof of concept and some visible successes to bring our team along. We were able to pick key agents of change among the chefs and lean on them to get involved. We saw some results and we shared our heartfelt stories of success.

With each young life transformed, more members of the Tender Greens team enlisted in the mission. An unexpected development was when a lot of our team members stepped out of the shadows and shared that they had come out of foster care. They knew well the challenges of growing up in foster care and could provide tremendous encouragement and mentorship to our students. They became tremendously valuable contributors to the success of SLP.

As our enrollment increased and daily management became more complex, we realized we needed someone on the Tender Greens management team with the expertise to direct the program. We made a key hire in Kevin Faist. Kevin had already spent a decade as a case manager at Homeboy Industries, a pioneering organization making positive change happen for thousands of formerly incarcerated gang members in East LA. He brought credibility and management expertise to our efforts.

We integrated the Sustainable Life Project team into our HR department to provide the support we already offered for all our existing team members. We put SLP into the HR budget, making it part of the regular HR workflow. We shared the care and attention for the interns with our entire staff and entrusted the day-to-day supervision to our chefs, with our nonprofit partners ready to assist as needed. Using this new structure, we professionalized the Sustainable Life Project, treating it as seriously as we did a new product or store launch.

The testimonials from Sustainable Life Project graduates proved useful for recruiting and member retention and became a valuable point of differentiation. Because of what the Sustainable Life Project accomplished, Tender Greens was viewed as more than just a restaurant. Sustainable Life graduates reinforced the sense of heart and community commitment that Tender Greens had aspired to from its inception.

There are so many stories of SLP transformations. Our graduates acquired new skills to advance in their jobs while we supported their growth and maturity as individuals. One measure of program success for us meant developing participants to become productive Tender Greens team members. Some stayed with us for many years while others found rewarding work with other companies. Another indicator of achievement was personal growth, which director Kevin Faist excelled at nurturing among SLP participants.

One such example comes to mind. Shortly after stepping aside as CEO, I visited our El Segundo restaurant. It was a pleasure to see many familiar faces and to meet enthusiastic new team members. A bright smile and a vaguely familiar voice greeted me with the news that he had been promoted to general manager. As I listened to his story of rising through the Tender Greens ranks I realized the proud professional before me was an early SLP participant. Years earlier she had come to us through the Orange County program with hopes of escaping her traumatic past.

The discovery that night that she had gone through identity transition while moving up the ranks at Tender Greens was incredibly moving to me. Proof that we could facilitate a path forward for foster youth stood in front of me—a young man full of poise and pride. What an amazing achievement for this graduate! And what a powerful story for the Tender Greens organization, inspiring them to stay committed to the transformative work of the Sustainable Life Project.

There's a common misconception that doing something "good" like the Sustainable Life Project means giving up profit margin. But the investment we made was ours to determine. We built it into the budget the same way you'd put in charitable contributions, but most importantly we could track and see the impact of our giving. How many kids do we want to move through the program in a year? What is the attrition rate likely to be? How much additional time will this represent for our HR staff and chefs? What we discovered is that the investment in the Sustainable Life Project was such a small number relative to our revenues, it was easy to scale.

Our larger goal was the adoption of this program by other companies. If we could get others to emulate us, we would scale impact beyond what we alone could accomplish. Many companies expressed interest, but it seems none followed through.

Finally, our experience showed us the importance of developing something that works within the rhythm of the organization, something woven into the daily routine of the business. The "let's all take a day off and clean up the beach" one-off style of impact just doesn't ring true and is not sustainable. It's a distraction, not a mission.

What we found genuinely sustainable was to build social change into our business with the same level of seriousness, the same commitment of resources, and the same determination to be successful as we would a new product, service, or location. It had to be built *into* our business, not bolted on with a quick release tab. The people and resources dedicated to social impact can't be seen as free-riding on the hard, revenue-generating work of the rest of the team members.

Chapter 10

The Next Phase: Professionalizing Our Business, Maintaining Our Purpose

"They always say time changes things, but you
actually have to change them yourself."
– *Andy Warhol*

*E*very business reaches the end of needed resources at various
stages of growth. How did we replenish essential resources, build
on what we had, add and subtract strategically? Often by listening
to others.

ACKNOWLEDGE AND RESOLVE INEVITABLE TENSIONS

Coming off the rush of successful multiple openings, we consulted
our roadmap. We had anticipated this stage of the business. We
had the revenue, we had the scale, and we had the growth trajectory. We'd gone through our first round of hard individual learning
and professional development. We knew we had to pivot opera-
tionally to continue our success. We just weren't sure how to get
there.

Adding layers of talent and creating more efficient systems had to be part of the plan. Frank Vizcarra's influence once again emerged.

David recalled his initial meeting with Frank, whose first exposure to Tender Greens had been as a guest in San Diego. Given his expertise as a McDonald's senior executive, Frank knew a thing or two about the hospitality industry. He was an early believer in Tender Greens' potential. At this introductory meeting, he let David know that "you're going to have a lot of work to do and it's going to be really hard. Going from three stores to five might seem tough. Getting to ten is nearly impossible." Frank's candor impressed us. We accepted the cash investment he offered, but more significantly, we signed on for an intense mentorship that would profoundly impact us and Tender Greens.

Until this juncture we had dabbled in systems creation, feedback, and continuous improvement. Seeing how the innovations Pete Balistreri introduced in San Diego could be exported to improve our other stores' operations demonstrated the value of standardizing some processes. Frank expanded our grasp of the value of systems. He introduced us to the interrelatedness of all things. That might sound quasi-spiritual or worse. But his cautionary tale was sobering—without a well-thought-out network of system design, implementation discipline, feedback loops, and creative destruction, eventually every company will collapse under the weight of its inefficiencies.

Once this decline takes hold, no one will have time to do the things that need to happen. Disunity, inconsistency, every man for himself, and destruction of the brand become the end game.

This level of systems thinking was foreign territory for us. On a superficial level, Matt and David could appreciate systems, standards, and feedback from a menu and recipe perspective. But underlying Frank's push for menu systems was his skepticism about whether we needed chefs. McDonald's was able to deliver a consistent product with only marginally skilled team members in their restaurants. The threat of systems thinking undermining or eliminating our culinary talent flared Erik's defenses. For Erik, taking chefs out of the Tender Greens formula was a non-starter.

As a chef himself, Erik had attracted highly skilled chefs to Tender Greens in part with the lure of creative freedom in their kitchens. Over time, when faced with the challenge of consistency for signature menu items as the stores multiplied across the state—the mashed potatoes had to be the same in San Diego as in Pasadena—Erik came to appreciate how some level of standardization could support, not constrain, the chefs. In time, Frank came to understand how the supply chain values and Erik's passion for chefs were essential to the Tender Greens ecosystem and success.

It wasn't just creative independence and culinary commitment that made Erik resistant to extensive systematization. Like many managers in large companies, he had been on the wrong end of systems initiatives that ended up disregarded in dusty binders. He'd witnessed layers of accountability being added in an effort to support management systems but coming at a cost to already heavily burdened operations teams. He'd seen how easily home office management gets bigger, flooding the field teams with "improvements." But Erik's distrust eventually yielded to Frank's insistence on implementing a *regulated* funnel of information and innovation—one or two improvements at a time, manageable changes, measured rollouts, and candid assessment.

We all saw the value in this approach. It would enable us to avoid the trap so many leaders fall into of setting overly ambitious goals for the first quarter, getting none of it done in the short term, then getting lost in the ensuing chaos as the rest of the year is spent recovering. The idea of thoughtfully vetting ideas and limiting the number of initiatives fit well with the Tender Greens focus on long-term thinking and perseverance. If we could design a process built on reliable feedback loops and honest communication, we believed, it would only help us thrive.

For David, the company was full of low-hanging fruit to practice systems thinking. But Frank helped him focus on more complex systems across our organization and held David accountable to keep chipping away at them: human resources practices and policies, training, bookkeeping and accounting, operations and facilities management protocols, and company communications.

As we got deeper into systems thinking and action, it made some things easier but it also made the business more complicated. Our teams had more deadlines and information to manage. New stresses and tensions arose. We viewed this as the natural tension between field operations and the home office. It's very similar to the front of the house and back of the house in restaurants. These groups speak two different languages and inhabit two different realities. When priorities collide and they can't find a way to agree, things get intense. As founders, we understood this tension yet it was something we had to resolve.

We had designed our business to be chef-centric. That meant our chefs had to be highly skilled culinarians and competent businesspeople. They already had the chef chops. It was our responsibility to give them the business tools and knowledge to manage their restaurants as profit centers.

Over time, we were training our chefs to think like owners, to be better managers of all their resources—not just the food but their teams, suppliers, and guests. We were asking them to practice a process Pete Balistreri so accurately described as "the balance of love and discipline—as chefs we have to love the team, the food, the guest, so honestly that you can taste the love. But we also have to have the discipline—controlling labor, food costs, human resources and other compliance needs—even though that isn't the fun part." Training the chefs was key to fulfilling our mission to become a sophisticated enterprise.

As we worked through this evolution, the partners' roles expanded as well.

Generally unflappable, Matt quietly found new ways to contribute his particular talents. As a chef, he was a great technician with a reliable palette and an engineer's mind for systems. His thoughtful approach to menu development meant we never lost sight of the regular Joe who just wanted good food. Matt's Southern roots found their way into our cooking—an irresistible combination of classic Southern flavors with California sensibilities. He would often challenge purism with a pragmatic perspective, bringing important balance as we grew beyond the early evangelists of chefs, foodies, and activists. In addition, Matt focused on the physical spaces of Tender Greens.

Erik played defense for our culinary team to protect them from burnout. He gently reminded the business side that the people in the field were the ones putting the ball through the hoop every day, making all our jobs possible. He worked to create sensitivity in the home office to avoid missteps, like calling a chef during the lunch rush to ask about their monthly inventory sheets.

David, meanwhile, was pressing the home office departments to collaborate and build better tools for the restaurants. The goal was greater accountability and systems compliance at the restaurant level. He defended the viability of the business by insisting on these as necessary practices.

We experienced the classic "creative" department versus "business" department conflict. Each is in a different headspace that attracts and needs different personality types. As founders we had to model the way to have constructive dialogue across these lines. To create a common language and a contract of sorts between all layers of the organization, we developed what came to be known as our Base Camp Principles. By agreeing to these statements as shared beliefs, we were agreeing to hold each other and ourselves accountable. Everyone at Tender Greens had a responsibility to call out those who weren't living up to them, while preserving mutual respect in all lines of communication.

Here is what came to be known as the "Legacy version" from our first effort to distill our beliefs.

BASE CAMP PRINCIPLES

OUR GOAL –

Restaurants people *really* love

– OUR COMMITMENT –

WE DELIVER INSPIRED FOOD, FRIENDLY SERVICE AND GREAT VALUE IN A COMFORTABLE SPACE.

Our menu reflects the best of the season and is prepared with simplicity, skill and passion. Every interaction is authentic, helpful, efficient, and kind.

Our guests are always excited to return soon and often.

Our restaurants are warm, relaxed, and sophisticated community hubs.

WE CHALLENGE OURSELVES, AND EACH OTHER, TO BE THE BEST.

Everybody is equally important to the mission.

We actively teach and learn from each other every day.

We value partnership, inspire passion, incubate good ideas, and celebrate innovation.

WE BALANCE OUR NEEDS WITH THOSE OF OUR STAKEHOLDERS SO THAT EVERYBODY WINS.

Our customers win because we provide an exceptional experience at a fair price.

Our team members win because we provide great jobs, opportunities for growth and the chance to discover their purpose and full potential.

Our farmers and other partners win because they can provide the best local products and services at a price that works for both of us.

Our investors win because we create local jobs, actively participate in and add value to the neighborhood and its culture.

Our environment wins because we make smart decisions that balance sustainable methods with the need for profitability.

WE STAY HUMBLE, GRATEFUL AND GIVE BACK IN MEANINGFUL WAYS.

We are thankful for our success and pay it forward whenever we can.

We could not afford to miss moments of empathy for every team member. We couldn't let a thoughtless call for inventory during a busy lunch get blown out of proportion, make tensions flare up, and send both sides into a tailspin. We had to demonstrate that what we asked of every team member and leader was sometimes for the good of the company and sometimes for the good of the individual.

For ourselves and our teams we created moments off-campus, away from the day-to-day demands, so we could stay heart-centered and connected about areas of conflict. These took many forms, such as a casual dinner in David's backyard or a relaxed retreat in Erik's living room. We offered instruction in mindfulness meditation conducted by a Buddhist monk and early morning Emotional Intelligence (EQ) sessions in the restaurants or at the home office. These EQ sessions provided safe spaces where team members could express strong emotions, hear each other's commonality, and choose more nurturing paths forward.

In the restaurants or at larger company gatherings, we implemented two-minute listening sessions at the start of team meetings—creating a valuable space before the "business agenda" for team members to speak about themselves and be listened to without judgment. We practiced expressing ourselves honestly and listening deeply. We asked people to say on a scale of 1-10 how they were feeling. This kind of sharing did more than relieve stress; it sometimes led to collaboration and creative solutions with one team member stepping up to help another.

Our person-centric culture found expression in various ways. Whether it was an acknowledgment exercise at the home office, a check-in before executive committee meetings, or calisthenics at the start of a restaurant shift, we encouraged our teams to devise ways to get and stay connected. When something really clicked at the restaurant or regional level, that practice would be shared company-wide. This reinforced our belief that human development and connection is as important as any business points covered in a meeting.

Over time the Base Camp Principles evolved to this essential version:

BASE CAMP

WHAT WE DO
we deliver inspired food, friendly service
and great value in a comfortable space

WHY WE DO IT
we believe that good food, whole food, real food
should be available to everyone, every day

HOW WE DO IT
we challenge ourselves, and each other, to
be the best

we balance our needs with those of our stakeholders
so that everybody wins

we stay humble, grateful and give back
in meaningful ways

Sometimes accidental magic happens, like the time we were refreshing our team member orientation program. David tapped Jonathan, a young graphic artist in our marketing department, to create an image showcasing the new Basecamp language. Jonathan took a playful approach, mixing fonts, weights and colors for a clean look. The unintended consequence is the magic. Combine and read the three phrases in bold---"Be the best so that everybody wins in meaningful ways."Jonathan's subconscious perfectly captured our philosophy, far more succinctly than all our previous efforts.

GET OUT OF YOUR OWN WAY. WELCOME IN TRUE BELIEVERS

Systems without sufficient people to execute get you nowhere. It was time to recruit additional talented people to solidify Tender Greens.

Thanks to our habitual frugality, including paying ourselves modestly, we were able to continually reinvest profits in the business. By 2011-12, we had the money to renovate our original Culver City restaurant. After five years of hard use, it needed more than a facelift—it needed additional capacity. The renovation provided us with an opportunity to enlarge our prep space by moving our offices out of the second floor and into a nearby post-war brick warehouse.

David set up our corporate office—affectionately dubbed "the home office"—which at this point was largely aspirational, i.e., a lot of space and desks occupied only by David and his assistant, Cristina Rodriguez. Occasionally, Erik might stop by if he was in the area. Matt sometimes came in to spread out blueprints for new locations. Our hope was to eventually populate this space with a team of business professionals.

After our first significant growth spurt in 2008-09, we had begun to outsource some key functions. We always looked for local service providers rather than national players, and for companies whose values and practices aligned with ours. We outsourced to up our game, avoid trouble and ensure we were following all the rules, regs and best practices in potentially vulnerable areas: bookkeeping and accounting, financial management, human resources, and public relations.

During this time, Lina O'Connor served as our outsourced controller and much more. We watched with admiration as she drove around to our restaurants, working one-on-one with our chefs. At monthly meetings Lina taught the chefs to understand their general ledger, interpret their profit and loss statement, and think like financial managers. She was also producing detailed reports that helped guide our business decisions. One day Lina told David, "I want to work for you guys and I think it's time for you to hire me." David recognized Lina as the first outside person to drink the Tender Greens Kool-Aid. In the summer of 2012, we brought her on as our full-time director of finance.

Until 2013 we had a "virtual" HR office handling compliance; our payroll processors served as a makeshift human resources information system (HRIS) and to pay team members. Once the complexity became untenable to manage in-house, we invited Cynthia Izaguirre Yilmaz to join the team as our first director of human resources.

Cynthia worked diligently to professionalize the HR function and ensure the fair, equitable, compliant, and happy work environment we envisioned. Human resources management requires a special kind of person—someone who understands all the complex, dynamic regulations, but can implement policies and support people with genuine caring. Cynthia had that rare combination of traits.

To drum up more opportunities for our brand to be featured, we hired Slife PR. Its owner, Kara Slife, introduced us to a professional level of public relations. She gave much needed focus and direction to our PR efforts.

As our PR needs grew, we moved on to a larger firm, JS², and then to the firm Murphy O'Brien. The constant behind these moves was Christina Wong. Christina was our account executive at

JS[2]. We liked working with her so much that when she moved to Murphy O'Brien, we followed as her client. During a planning session for our annual PR campaign, Christina asked Erik when we were intending to bring someone in-house. Erik said, "We don't need anybody in-house. We've got you." "Exactly," Christina replied. We continued to work with her as a client until her contract expired. Then she joined our team.

In creating our unique local, regional, and sustainable supply chain, Erik and Matt had developed close relationships with our suppliers. As Erik's responsibilities supporting the restaurants grew, he began to realize that a sentimental attachment to maintaining his personal relationships with small suppliers was becoming unsupportable. And Matt's role leading real estate development was all-consuming. In 2015, Michael Antoci, the same guy who helped connect us with boutique meat suppliers in our earliest days, took on a greater role managing and extending our supply chain. We trusted Michael to grow Tender Greens supply chain while adhering to our clearly defined principles and standards.

We now had professional depth in finance, human resources, public relations, and supply chain management. On the technology side, Jason Buehler, owner of Cerge, added tremendous value. Jason continued the work begun by Brad Akerman, our first IT professional, of systematizing store-level and company-level IT. Jason helped us understand how technology might streamline our processes and enhance hospitality.

With this foundation of home office professionals, we began to build field support for operations by naming regional managers. Once a region reached three units with the potential for five, we promoted our strongest local chef to a regional role. As owners, we were now managing the managers with strong leaders across the regions. We were working on the business but not *in* the business every day. Or as we expressed it, we had layers between us and the 9-1-1 calls.

This was a time of profound change for us. David was freed from the relentless daily demands of accounting and human resources management. With the experience and input contributed by Cynthia, Christina, and Lina, he was executing on Frank Vizcarra's advice to look at the interconnectedness of all things.

David formed a planning team whose role was to continuously build better mousetraps—to cut down on steps, automate, develop, and implement systems. As a group we were coming up with improved training programs, identifying better reporting software, inventing and refining as the company continued to evolve. David's job became managing the planning team—getting everyone together regularly for productive sessions with agendas, managing our strategic plans, and managing our personalities.

There were cultural elements to infuse and protect within this group too—what we thought of as the spiritual elements that had always been part of Tender Greens. We purposefully worked to foster understanding of and appreciation for each other, having occasional dinners together, and sharing who we were outside of work.

For Erik, things changed significantly too. He had gotten over his distrust for Frank's systems thinking and was meeting with him on a monthly basis. He became Frank's mentee, much as David had earlier. During this time, Frank's counsel helped Erik put aside his tendency to over-value some previously held opinions. He felt free to get out of his own precious way and develop the vocabulary for business at scale. It went beyond systems thinking; it was *strategic* thinking, delivered by Frank in his lowkey style as a trusted advisor—our "guide on the side."

Erik embraced the larger role of managing the regional managers rather than individual restaurants. He tried to maintain close connections to all the chefs without "getting in the weeds"—showing interest in and support for the chefs, while allowing the regional managers to run their own teams. There were always team members who would come directly to one or another of the founders, but mostly we succeeded in creating some buffering layers.

The benefits of David's planning team were becoming evident. As the complexity of the business increased, the tools to manage it evolved. As Lina continued building out financial reporting and administrative systems, chef managers began to see greater results through better business insight. Each of the regions began to develop their own hierarchy of leadership. By sharing standards and performance transparently across the company, they were able to measure their results against other regions and restaurants.

Increasingly Erik and Matt could collaborate on expansion and real estate development. Erik emerged as the partner best suited to doing outward facing events with community, press, and other events. He started to collaborate as a colleague with other brand founders, first in California and subsequently on a national basis. Through this expanded professional network he made friends, shared notes, and tapped into a collective consciousness, gaining insights into successes and challenges of others in our industry. Participating in this peer group was both intensely competitive and supportive. Erik was able to borrow ideas and traits—as well as enjoy the positive influence of—those whom he admired.

NEVER LET GO OF YOUR CORE VALUES

We and our teams did not get through the professionalizing of our company without pain, misjudgments, and outright mistakes. For example, we decided to launch an events and catering business in response to high demand. We made the right decision to hire a seasoned events person from the Patina group to run it, but we made a poor choice to produce the food from our restaurant kitchens and try to compete with the established high-end caterers like Wolfgang Puck, Heirloom LA, and Patina Group.

The real miss was that we could not deliver on our core value proposition. We discovered that trying to deliver comparable quality with the necessary level of service refinement but at a lower price point failed to achieve enough profitability to justify the effort. It was both a distraction and a wrong direction for the business.

What helped us course correct was to return to our foundations—our respect for one another and our commitment to grow together, not apart. We were always anchored in this mutual respect and what we recognized as "the power of three." A solo founder is at risk of isolation. Two founders are often mired in unresolvable disputes. Three founders with complementary skills who have the power to sway one another was central to our success.

To take advantage of this power of three, each of us had to get over our knee-jerk reactions in the moment. To really hear each other's message. In moments of partner tension we would often playfully ask each other, "Do you need a nap? Do you need a hug?" We could not afford to lose sight of our identity first as people with deep mutual interdependence.

There is of course the reality of business. To quote Pete Balistreri again, "the balance of love and discipline." As we struggled to professionalize, we had to commit to adherence to a code borrowed from Frank—WW/WN/HDWFI. Translated that means "What's working, what's not, and how do we fix it?" This process of "creative destruction" helped us avoid the trap of falling in love with our brand. Sound advice came from Michael Mack, founder of the Souplantation, who encouraged us to throw rocks at our business every day and to work hard at trying to anticipate what might put us out of business.

We held feedback sessions with regularity in an environment of trust and respect so that hard truths could be spoken at all levels of the organization. We did it with the planning team, but it was trickier with regionals and the planning team together, because we were constantly working to overcome a certain level of distrust. We knew that we could only get through it if we talked about everything openly. It is never easy to get everybody in a room to fix a problem and come away with a winning feeling. We didn't want the restaurants to mistrust the expanding home office or resent the planning team. And we certainly didn't want the home office team to underestimate the dedication and talent of the chefs.

Passions run high when your teams are engaged. We'd work to lower the temperature of emotions a bit and remind everyone of our common goal—we all want what's best for the company. You can't expect team members to be guided by what's best for the company if they don't know what is going on in the company. We owed it to our team members to be transparent in all aspects of Tender Greens operations.

An important element of transparency addresses career opportunity. We believed in bringing people up from within the ranks. To demonstrate that, mature homegrown talent earned the opportunity to manage their own restaurants. Seeing successes led to formalizing our manager-in-training (MIT) program, derived in part from the powerful apprenticeship system Pete Balistreri pioneered in San Diego.

As a company we committed to designing a clear career ladder from entry level positions to executive chef. No matter how you became part of Tender Greens, there was a potential path to running your own restaurant. We encouraged internal mentorship so those who had been part of our early stage growth were able to grab somebody's hand to pull them along. One hand upwards asking for help and guidance, a hand to your back helping the next person to the next level. That was our vision, profoundly influenced by Abraham Maslow's "hierarchy of human needs." Maslow showed that the key to human motivation lies in recognizing five levels of need: physiological, safety, love and belonging, esteem, and self-actualization.

Our values encouraged us to chart a growth map for individuals within our company. We wanted to show everyone in our organization what their next step would look like—including promotions to regional manager, director or even VP. We wanted everybody to know what the timeline was, what the markers were, and the competency expectations for a move up to that next level.

This transparency created a culture of competition that was often positive, but at times was not. Our restaurants would pay close attention to each other's Instagram accounts and call each other out if something looked "like hash". At times, the pressure for bragging rights about food cost or revenue growth led chefs to shave corners. We had to balance incentivizing with supervising, making sure goals were attainable without compromising quality or brand integrity. Sharing the innovations and successes openly among the teams was just another creative tension we had to manage as we matured. Keeping the culture focused not on beating others but on contributing to our collective success.

There was cool stuff happening—in professionalizing we hadn't become just like any business—we were teaching mindfulness and doing emotional intelligence classes for the teams. We might have a Buddhist monk come to bless the restaurants. We saw beautiful stuff when the teams went deep. We were trying to behave as a thoroughly sophisticated company without letting go of our goal—that every team member would say, "This is the best job I have ever had."

Building company infrastructure and evolving into our executive roles during this stage of Tender Greens' internal growth was part of our practice and preparation. We had our original partners' agreement and our shared core values to serve as our True North. An important part of that was our commitment to patient growth. To reach the next plateau we would have to look externally. Adding necessary intellectual, human, and financial capital required careful curation of an advisory board. This was our next challenge as founders.

Chapter 11

Adding Intellectual Capital: Forming the Advisory Board

"Who you are surrounded by often determines who you become."
– Vicky Saunders

*E*ntrepreneurs fret about having enough money, but often don't worry enough about having sufficient brain power. Engaging smart people who will move your organization forward without staging a coup or trying to make you abandon your ideals takes maturity, wisdom, humility, and patience.

We were fortunate to build an advisory team who brought the tremendous power of their expertise to our goals and vision. This was a crucial stage in scaling our enterprise.

TALENTED PEOPLE WANT TO HELP YOU

There's an especially meaningful section in Howard Schultz's book "Pour Your Heart Into It" when he confesses to a vulnerability most of us have. For entrepreneurs, it can be painful to admit what you don't know. It's even more painful to admit it to someone who has greater experience and wisdom. Our fear centers on being revealed as incompetent or at least as a poser who is working hard to appear to be a confident professional. One of a founder's greatest fears is being told by someone they admire, "Wow, you really have no idea what you're doing."

Schultz overcame his reluctance to seek advice and things obviously worked out for him. David remembers reading these passages and filing them away for when the right moment happened with Tender Greens.

As partners, we were honest with each other about the point when we, individually and collectively, had passed beyond what our previous experience had trained us for. Although we hadn't mapped out the timelines for when this would happen, we could imagine inviting input in stages from a group of seasoned professionals— paid consultants, mentors, an advisory board, and a formal board of directors.

We felt we could better focus our needs and find the right people with the necessary resources if we took it one stage at a time. Incremental professional growth would enable us to solve a greater range of problems faster: We would gain confidence at managing the power dynamics in each type of relationship, especially as these relationships resulted from larger investments.

Initially we sought ad hoc advice from various professionals whom we hired on an as-needed basis. The first stage of structured mentorship happened when Frank Vizcarra sought us out. As we mentioned previously, after dining at the Tender Greens in San Diego, he was so impressed that he became an early investor. As trust and understanding built between us, Frank helped us move to the next level of external engagement by guiding us in the establishment of an advisory board.

In 2013, we chose to form an advisory board for a number of reasons. Technically, we already had a founder's board of directors consisting of the three of us, created when we formed our T.Y.P. Restaurant Group, Inc. but that was a board mostly in name only. One or two early investors periodically pressured us with questions about forming a board that would include them. Rather than just ignoring them, we reached out to other founders like Rick Federico at P.F. Chang's and Rick Rosenfield, one of the California Pizza Kitchen founders, for their advice, which was: don't expand your formal board until you have to.

Investigating what it meant to professionalize our board with non-founders as directors, we encountered too many hurdles. For starters, we couldn't afford to pay the sort of people we would want in that role. The idea that directors would have fiduciary responsibility, that we'd need directors & officers insurance, and that they'd have genuine oversight authority was too much, too soon for our partnership and business.

An advisory board seemed much more palatable as a next step. Members of an advisory board would serve at the invitation of the founders. They would have no fiduciary responsibility or authority. There was no obligation to compensate them. We could offer advisors a small grant of stock options if we wanted to. It was our decision to choose people we felt comfortable with. Following Frank's advice, we felt ready to include more people in our circle of trust. It would buy us time before expanding our formal board of directors. At the same time, we could build relationships that would give us access to the information, experience, and proven solutions we lacked.

BE STRATEGIC IN WHOM YOU SELECT

Frank laid out a straightforward formula to help shape our advisory board—"Find five people who have already been where you're trying to go and make sure each of them is good at different things." We added a filter of our own—is this someone we want to sit across the table from over lunch? That might sound frivolous, but for us it meant being comfortable, values aligned, and able to speak the same language.

Michael Mack, founder of Souplantation, was one of our early picks. Michael had been successful as a consultant with Bain Capital in Boston before launching his food business. He had grown Souplantation and taken it public. He knew firsthand what it meant to grow to the IPO stage. He understood all the levels and how it changed his life and the company. We wanted that wisdom at our table. Michael was a strong proponent of John Mackey's belief system of "conscious capitalism." He also spoke to our spiritual heart center while adding tremendous depth to our financial education.

One day Erik got a call from Joachim Splichal, founder of the Patina Group and a chef entrepreneur whose career Erik had followed with admiration and respect. Joachim had been frequenting the Pasadena Tender Greens with his sons and really enjoyed it. He wanted to meet with Erik about the business. No question, this was someone Erik wanted to have lunch with.

Joachim had built the Patina Group into a thriving empire in fine dining, with diverse business lines reaching into off-premises catering and sports arena food service. With his stellar background as a fine dining chef, he was the advisor closest to our pedigree. He had sold his company then bought it back and he did it with elegance in a way we could appreciate. Much to Erik's delight, over lunch Joachim planted the seed that he would be interested in helping us in any way. Given that he was able to command $1,000 an hour as a restaurant consultant, we clearly could not afford to hire him. Happily, we were able to offer him a place on our advisory board. Joachim was extraordinarily helpful along our journey. His credibility and credentials added a welcome "chef/founder" voice to the group.

Don Laden was another one of Frank's introductions, so in a sense he was pre-vetted. Unlike Michael and Joachim, Don became a Tender Greens investor, representing the family office of the former owners of the IAMS pet food company. Besides being a really nice guy, Don had been the VP of Marketing for IAMS. Since we were deficient in marketing expertise, his perspective was a welcome addition to the mix.

By bringing these three executives onto our advisory board, we'd recruited people who had done what we hoped to do but in different segments and in different ways—Michael from fast casual with financial sophistication around IPOs; Joachim from scale with fine dining quality; Don with marketing chops and a network beyond hospitality. Our inner circle now had a blend of roles—Frank and Don as representatives of investors; Michael and Joachim as what USHG's Danny Meyer referred to as "helpful uncles." They had no financial stake in the business. They were not there to protect their money interests but to help a company they believed in and founders they liked.

When building an advisory group, it can be tempting to fill these spots with enthusiastic investors. What we came to realize was that our investors were already in our corner. We'd be wasting our chips if we brought in investors simply because they wanted to help or keep a closer eye on their money.

Building our advisory board with the right independent businesspeople connected us to folks we wanted in our corner, such as wise professionals like Joachim whom we could never afford to pay. Because they believed in us, they'd accept the occasional great lunch as payment—coupled with the satisfaction of seeing us succeed.

Our vetting process required us to honestly assess how each individual would be helpful to our mission. Will they put the best interests of the company first? Do we want to have this close a relationship with them? If we all agreed, then it came down to being bold enough to ask, "Will you be our advisor?" We were careful about who we approached. No one turned us down.

Once this advisory board was in place, we had access to a much deeper pool of wisdom from investors and "helpful uncles." They offered visibility around the corners. It made for a potent group of elders who had been there and back. If they had strong opinions we should listen to them. That's what they're there for. Ultimately, it was up to us as founders and as the voting board to determine what would result in the betterment of the company and the brand. We never felt we were answering to or working for this advisory board. It was a very positive experience that significantly promoted our growth as a business and as business leaders.

HONOR THEIR EXPERTISE. VALUE THEIR TIME

To set us up for success, we invested the time and effort to draw up a formal agreement for our advisory board. This was a way to clarify expectations for all parties—the anticipated time commitment, what resources we wanted from them, what we'd offer in return. No surprises, misunderstandings, or resentment. It took a bit of courage on our part to put our cards on the table.

As compensation, we proposed granting some options. Honestly at this point we didn't fully understand the implications of options, but we felt it made it possible for our advisors to participate in our growth. They knew we couldn't be writing big checks to reward them for their counsel. What we found was, especially for the "helpful uncles," they were betting on the rider and not the horse. More than making money, they just wanted to give us meaningful help.

We did not put any pressure on our advisory board to invest, though they had a first look at each next capital raise—how much and from whom. They had the same opportunity to participate as any team member with visibility of the offer but no obligation to invest. Every advisor signed our agreement, although in some cases there was first a bit of haggling over options.

No group of advisors, no matter how talented and well-intentioned, can help you if you don't tell them what you need. This was an exercise for the three of us; before each advisory session we'd sit down together and write out what we were struggling with. To get the maximum value from our meetings, we shared our specific questions in advance so our advisors showed up ready to help. We tried to use the advisory board to solve one or two big challenges that we weren't able to get through on our own, or at least that we'd feel more confident about with their guidance. Busy professionals don't want to spend their time listening to you go over reports. Give them problems to solve. There's more value for both sides in meetings that are focused on solutions.

We disciplined ourselves to conduct these advisory meetings with utmost professionalism. Thoughtful agendas were circulated in advance. All necessary documentation was provided as context. We stuck to our agendas, managed the clock, kept things moving. We tabled things that needed to be revisited rather than derailing us from the rest of the topics. These behaviors kept our advisors engaged because we made it possible for them to genuinely contribute.

The time between meetings is a valuable resource, which we learned to mine for more connections and advice. Our advisors were willing to open doors for us with key introductions or provide us with instructive examples, templates or other materials from their companies. At the same time, we were careful not to treat our advisors as our team members. We recognized the need to be lean and intentional in our communications with them between meetings, not to ask too much of their time and attention.

We used an approach from a Seth Godin talk about how to get the most value from anyone who is willing to help you. It goes back to clarity and transparency. What "hat" do you want them to wear? What lane is theirs? Why have you given them these specific roles? Be consistent about what you ask and of whom you ask it. These roles can evolve and change but the clearer you are on the job description for particular board members, the more readily and confidently they can contribute in their own voice and from their unique place at the table.

Getting comfortable with high-level professionals who both challenged and supported us proved to be an important growth step for us as founders. Later, as the business matured and more sophisticated money came in, our formal board of directors' participation carried more influential weight. In the meantime, with our advisors' input, we were executing on our long-term vision with more confidence and a clearer view of how to prepare for what lay ahead.

One striking example of the value we derived from our advisors was their coaching about taking on a sizable equity investor. Meeting notes from that session formed the basis for the long litany of questions and concerns we generated before we entertained any serious negotiations. Each of our advisors weighed in from their "lane" of expertise. They asked us to figure out what our deal breakers were, what we needed vs. what someone might offer, how much control we were willing to surrender, and how we were going to protect our organization from a "people perspective." They wanted clear, thoughtful answers from us, not off-the cuff-responses. It got us thinking and talking among ourselves in a frank and focused way. As a result we were much better positioned to be proactive and aligned when investors came calling.

Our advisors understood that part of the long view was the importance of protecting our company culture. We wanted to ensure that the values and practices we built the company on would remain deeply rooted in Tender Greens well into the future.

Chapter 12

Staying Focused: Best-in-Class Problems

"If you're trying to create a company, it's like baking a cake.
You have to have all the ingredients in the right proportions."
–Elon Musk

We had worked very hard to get to the top, and now we were there (almost). This was no time to coast. We found we had to cling even tighter to the practices that had brought success, and to not be seduced by the many shiny objects likely to come our way. Dealing with success, it turns out, was its own difficult business problem.

WHEN BUSINESS GETS HARDER, DON'T LOOK FOR THE EASY WAY FORWARD

Up until this point, we've shared the lessons we learned mostly based on what we got right. Not always on the first try, but after listening to solid advice, then making adjustments and adaptations. Sometimes this was relatively easy. Other times, painful.

In this chapter, we describe what we learned by doing a number of things wrong—not out of carelessness or laziness; we were all still working extremely hard. Each in our own way believed we were doing what was necessary to secure the company's future. But increased competition and what we began to perceive as declining store operations were a wakeup call that led us to a course correction.

From 2011 through 2014, we were well on our way to reaching our growth and performance goals for Tender Greens. But as is often the case with first movers, our success spawned a wave of imitators. Private equity, sensing opportunity, started to drive growth in the fast casual sector. Newcomers poured in—Sweetgreen, Flowerchild, Mendocino Farms, Lemonade. In Santa Monica, we went from being the only ones on the block to being surrounded by a dozen concepts with three salad options and more. They were all pretty good. The stakes had been upped and the competition was figuring it out. The fight for market share was intense.

At the same time, real estate prices were increasing. And with a boom in the restaurant sector, the labor market was getting tighter. It was harder to find affordable locations, harder to attract talent at all levels to operate our restaurants. Smart competition, more costly real estate, and a thinning labor pool threatened to put the brakes on our ability to expand.

We were concerned that every Tender Greens opening came with an expectation of very high performance, beginning at a breakeven of $1.5 million in revenue. We had enough restaurants by this point to realize that it was going to be very hard to grow our company with the existing Tender Greens footprint and operations plan as our model. The significant changes in the market made us feel that opportunity in our traditional venues was disappearing. We began to think our best option for opening more restaurants was to open something different. The easiest path to growth seemed to be in smaller markets, not the increasingly high-priced urban centers where we were already well established.

Work started on the development of a concept we named Little Gem (not to be confused with the San Francisco restaurants currently operating under that name). The idea was to build a scaled-down, even more affordable version of Tender Greens without diluting the brand. We were designing Little Gem to be less expensive to build and operate. Faster service, lower prices, fewer staff, more limited selections but still high quality. The restaurants we envisioned were compact spaces in suburban locations—smaller markets that couldn't support the high guest traffic we needed for a traditional Tender Greens to be viable. We even considered taking over dying fast-food drive-through locations. This was our first swing at how we could reduce complexity and still deliver on our brand value proposition.

We started menu and concept development for the Little Gem line. We remember the day we presented the pitch deck at a meeting with Clay Mathile, former CEO of IAMS. We launched into the concept while Clay glared at us wordlessly. Suddenly he slammed his powerful fists onto the table. "You've got this jewel of a brand that requires all your attention. Why are you creating this distraction? Stop. Right now." He didn't just mean our presentation. He meant the whole concept. And he was right.

Others had warned us that Little Gem would distract us. Each of us felt that. But we didn't know what else would enable us to grow. We figured smaller, simpler stores were the answer, though we also sensed a risk of brand dilution.

Meanwhile, in 2014 our newest group of restaurants was underperforming on a lot of levels. We hadn't made the best real estate choices. In some cases we had overbuilt. Some were too expensive to run. Store leadership and staff were not up to our standards. Making the rounds to locations we couldn't help admitting, "Shit... we have some restaurants that are not cutting it. We need to get back in the game."

KEEP YOUR BEST PEOPLE CLOSE TO YOUR GUESTS AND YOUR PRODUCT

During this time we were within field goal range of completing our Ten Year Plan. We had nearly built what we said we were going to build. We started positioning ourselves for what would become a deal. That meant we had put our active roles in operations and business management on cruise control a little bit. Conversations with interested equity investors were starting to develop. We were spending a lot of time and energy working on externalities.

As partners we had fallen back into silos of our own creation. Matt was relying heavily on the design teams and construction firms he had assembled. He was trying to value engineer construction elements to a kit of parts. The results seemed to indicate that we'd lost our design way. The build outs didn't get cheaper, and too often the architects and designers were making choices that didn't feel or look right. The disappointing result was restaurants that sometimes seemed over built, over designed, too corporate or even chain- restaurant style. And weren't less costly to build.

Erik was on the road much of the time trying to elevate Tender Greens from a leading California name to a prominent national brand. He was making the rounds as a speaker at conferences, cultivating media contacts, and gaining influential national exposure for us. His participation in industry events exposed what was an intense battle—new brands with heavy financing and smart marketing angles were imitating what we'd invented and grabbing bits of credit for it. The successes and insights were valuable. However, all the travel and time away came at the cost of Erik's increased separation from the Tender Greens operations teams.

David was managing the home office business center while maintaining the many external relationships necessary to provide the capital fueling our growth. He had the challenges of balancing senior management's career ambitions, the tensions and expectations of lenders, and the complexities and weight of the statewide organization. We thought we had built the infrastructure necessary to support the company but cracks in the foundation were becoming evident.

To manage growth, to take ourselves out of day-to-day operations, and to create advancement opportunities for our most talented team members, we had been promoting high-performing people to regional management positions. The "regionals" served multiple critical roles. They were watchdogs for quality control, teachers and trainers in the field, cultivators of talent, and emergency first responders when any of their restaurants needed help. We could not have continued to grow the business without their expertise and energetic dedication to our team.

Rick Federico from P.F. Chang's had warned us to avoid creating silos and multiple management layers—"Always keep your best people closest to your guests and your product." But keeping your most ambitious and talented people close to the guest is tough—the burnout factor of daily operations is real. And often the proven way to keep great people in your company is by encouraging them to ascend the career ladder.

We came to realize that when we hire people who are driven by career, we have to honor their need for development. There are also very valuable people who are good at what they do and want to stay in the same position, close to the customer and reliable contributors to daily operations. Those individuals need to be incentivized to stay put. The challenge is finding ways to keep them excited about and gratified by their work. Remove the temptation to leave, possibly by giving them more autonomy and certainly by regularly recognizing the work they do. The pressure to satisfy our more ambitious staff and retain our solid line workers only grew more intense over time.

It had taken everything we had as partners and professionals to run and grow Tender Greens to this point. By 2014-2015 we were at risk of being the Old School brand outpaced by newcomers. Having been so focused on the future, we lost sight of the details that had formed the basis of our value proposition.

SUCCESS IS ALWAYS IN THE DETAILS

During rapid expansion, we'd gone through a period of creating some restaurants that were underperforming. We began to talk about the dangerous idea of being "good enough"—which should have been a major "red flag."

With so much more competition, we had to admit that customers might decide to frequent a restaurant down the block because it was closer, less crowded, maybe a bit more convenient—small trade-offs they were willing to make because they—the competitor—were "good enough." We had to rally everyone on our team to embrace our mantra that Tender Greens had to be more—we had to be *special.*

How do you protect your brand when it is under assault from new market entrants? By revisiting what made you special in the first place. By leaning into your unique qualities. We stressed to all our team members that Tender Greens had to deliver more to our customers—service that was friendly, professional, and fast; food that was consistently fresh and delicious. Our special qualities had to make our customers believe no substitute would be "good enough" for them. We had to communicate our difference powerfully to our guests. We had to reliably deliver on that promise.

Our brand-protecting moat, our superpower, was our culinary talent. Nobody else had it. Competitors were staffing their stores with line cooks and prep people; our stores were managed by highly skilled chefs. We put real money into that talent. It was an investment others weren't willing to make. With our culinary expertise, we could innovate in real time at the store level on a daily basis.

It became trendy for many restaurants to claim they were using locally sourced products. They would claim to have a sustainable, chef-driven supply chain but they couldn't compare to ours. Unlike our competitors, Tender Greens could be fully transparent about our wide, deep, and authentically local supply chain. The combination of our close supplier relationships and our chef talent meant we were able to take advantage of unique ingredients for seasonal excitement—like purple rutabaga, ramps, and specialty mushrooms. You could depend on Tender Greens to keep food ideas fresh and exciting.

We could beat the competition on these counts. But not without management effort. Our complexity made consistency a challenge at times. Sometimes chefs went off on a tangent. Our job as founders was to get everyone in the organization back to fundamentals. Taste the soup. Sample the mashed potatoes. See the restaurant as your guests see it. These would be our strongest weapons to protect market share while continuing to drive the volume of traffic in each store.

From an investment perspective, one of our unique qualities was our AUV (Average Unit Volume). Beginning with our first Culver City location we had achieved numbers that were virtually unheard of in the industry—$3.8 million was our benchmark. We were able to afford "Main on Main" store locations because of the volumes we were doing. Our competitors couldn't match us. As we began to consider our exit strategy, preserving these outstanding figures was essential.

The conversation about how to revive our standards started with us. We initiated a process of rallying the entire company with a call to action at the highest levels—a challenge to the regionals to reclaim being special. We urged them to convey this critical message to their teams.

We couldn't dismantle the structure of the organization, but we could dedicate ourselves to getting closer to our team members and our product. To initiate this effort, David and Erik launched our "Train the Trainer Tour." We made a commitment to go to every restaurant and spend a full day with the up-and-coming supervisors and managers-in-training. We'd go through training standards but equally important we would get to know our team members. After such rapid growth, we had not met many store staff. As founders, we wanted to establish that relationship and human connection. Rather than being faces on the website, we took this opportunity to be known by all the teams and get closer to key people.

Our presentation was designed to empower participants. We'd open the session with a blank sheet of flip chart paper and say to the staff, "Tell us all the problems you have right now. What are the things that make it hard for you to do a great job? It's our goal to address each one of these today."

We'd run through our presentation about food and service standards, about learning and motivating staff. We made sure to weave into our presentation their list of obstacles so at the end we could go back to that flip chart page, take a black marker and cross them off. We'd take the feedback back to the regionals and the home office and say, "These are the things we need to fix." Field-generated problems got put on the action plan for resolution. Then we held our leaders accountable to follow through, down to the store level.

We remember one session in particular in San Francisco. We felt we were really connecting with this team of young kids, feeling like the best possible dads as the team members got into the rhythm of the class. Caught up in the spirit of inclusion, we decided on the fly to invite them all to join us for dinner at Yuet Lee, our favorite Chinese restaurant. Suddenly everyone got busy on their cell phones. No takers. Somewhat deflated, we made our way to the restaurant only to find it was closed that night. The gods had intervened to spare us the embarrassment.

In retrospect, we did nothing extraordinary in our drive to preserve what was special about Tender Greens. It's always about the basics. By focusing our attention too much on the future, we lost sight of this fundamental truth. Seduced by our successes, we fell a bit under the spell of believing our own headlines. That's always dangerous. It's fantastic when Conde Nast singles you out in a global market. But in a way, that only intensifies the expectations and the pressure to deliver.

This time, we were able to recover. Up ahead, more changes in the industry were coming our way, bringing new challenges to our business.

Chapter 13

Getting Schooled in Finance: Positioning Our Company for Value

"Capital is that part of wealth which is
devoted to obtaining further wealth."
– *Alfred Marshall*

In 2014 markets were moving. Valuations were high and we were at the top of our game. It was time to move. Our preparation for this moment started years earlier. We'd begun meeting with money people—watching, listening, and learning about what serious investors looked for. Because of these sometimes painful experiences, we felt ready to quietly start taking big money meetings.

VALUATION IS BOTH EMOTION AND MATH

There's no denying it takes money to grow a business. The options for raising capital and the consequences each choice entails are often big unknowns for founders. They certainly were for us. We were simultaneously trying to run the business, scale the business, and figure out how to sell the business.

We built our Ten Year Plan with the end in mind—a liquidity event. But honestly we had no idea what that might look like. How did we determine our company valuation? What did we need to do along the way to build to the most favorable valuation? Which of these potential paths to growth and value should we pursue—self-funding, bank debt, ongoing rounds of equity raises, courting larger investors, franchising, or even ultimately taking Tender Greens public? We asked these questions early on and repeatedly to help guide our financial strategy.

We'd already seen the benefit of identifying mentors and advisors. It was a natural step to seek professional financial advice from people we could trust—people with a lot more experience. Pretty quickly we learned that big banks were mostly interested in selling us services like credit card processing. Regional banks were less encumbered by a bunch of "NO" policies. They were more excited about supporting smaller businesses and seemed to exercise more autonomy to make decisions. The most helpful individuals were small, regional bankers and investment professionals, starting with Bob Franko at Beach Business Bank.

By the time we had three stores, we were getting nowhere talking to Bank of America about a commercial loan. Bob took a different approach. He opened up the whiteboard in his office and said, "Let me teach you about valuation, debt, and banking relationships." It was like watching Shark Tank before Shark Tank existed.

Bob's tutorial on the roles and relationships of finance started us thinking as businesspeople. We now had some insights into using the right math and the right vocabulary to talk to more sophisticated parties. Later we'd make fun of all the insider lingo, "opening the kimono, drilling down, circling back, on the platform." But for now, this new information opened a critical pathway to understanding more about the routes to growth and building valuation.

To gain these insights, we had to be open about our financial position and business. We asked for NDAs (non-disclosure agreements) before proceeding and nobody had a problem with that. There are two sides to the value equation in these conversations. We were meeting with experienced lenders and investors who were looking at a lot of new business concepts. Our niche in the restaurant business was still emerging so they had nothing to compare us to. By sharing our information, we gave an investment banker insight into this new, potentially explosive business sector. He or she could confidently use this information to explore other deals without naming us. In exchange, the banker gave us examples of current valuations in a range of other restaurants. Their advice—we needed to improve our EBITDA (earnings before interest, taxes, depreciation, and amortization) especially at the store level (often called "4-Wall"). That became a number we started to focus on. One immediate consequence was the outsourcing of our accounting to Vine Solutions. They could provide a more professional set of financial statements than we could produce internally.

To fund growth, you have to weigh the risks and rewards. In self-funding, the risk is you can't raise enough money to cover commitments. This would slow growth. The reward is that you hold on to more, you're more frugal and you retain control. By acquiring debt, you can build a loaded balance sheet that enables you to take advantage of opportunities without the distraction of raising capital. Finding the right mix is key.

If you take on debt through a government-supported program like the Small Business Administration (SBA) the bank is going to get its money back. Since the government backs these loans, they provide affordable money to the borrower with little risk to the lender. Your lender can be, as Bob Franko was, calm, disciplined, and supportive. On the other hand, equity investors might be more aggressive. It's always useful to have at least one patient, conservative voice in the investment mix.

To avoid selling more equity, we opted for debt through SBA loans. Our first SBA loan was just over $1 million. We were subsequently able to acquire multiple rounds of SBA loans through our regional bank. The advice to use debt rather than equity was straightforward—if you're confident in your ability to repay the loan, stop selling any more equity until you've driven up the company valuation. The SBA loans made this possible.

The next round of capital raise would be much larger—going outside our close circle of friends, family, and guests to more sophisticated investors with a greater need to satisfy their requirements for returns. One of our more helpful early investors and somebody we'll always consider a friend was Andy Skov. He generously introduced us to food space investors like Chris Hemmeter, who in turn referred us to industry advisors and private equity dealmakers like David Jacquin and Mark Saltzgaber. Although we were too small and too early stage for private equity, Mark advised us on our preliminary financial model. We were preparing to do an offering to raise $1.5 million. We wanted some outside perspective to reassure us that it was the right amount. Mark coached us to make sure our accounting was consistent, organized, and presented us in the right light. Once we had that together, he made additional introductions to help us build our network. We took a lot of information meetings, gathering more insights and confidence with each one.

You must have a sound financial model to go after larger investments, and many founders get that. But what is easy to miss is the importance of truly understanding the value of what you have to sell.

Because we based our business on a long, patient growth concept, we always had clarity about what we were building. Early investors could align with that vision. In the startup days, it was more emotion than math. We were presenting somewhat arbitrary numbers because there were no publicly traded companies to compare with. Private companies' financial performances were not readily available. We based our valuation on 1.5 times revenue and that seemed fair. Our early investors weren't overly critical. They would read the story of our brand, see our projections, and say, "that sounds good." With these smaller raises, we were selling equity in the company to patient money—i.e., investors willing to stay with us as we grew.

As the business matured and our capital rounds got bigger, we had to learn to describe more specifically what we were promising to investors. It's easy to confuse what you want and need as a founder with what your investor wants and needs. We had to figure out how to achieve the best outcome for ourselves and all our investors.

We couldn't know how much capital to raise until we had a forecasting model to show what the company would need to fuel growth at a projected rate—that's the math part. If we raised more than we needed, there might be pressure to grow prematurely. That can cause its own set of problems. Frank Vizcarra recommended we work with Bob Franko and Chuck Stevens, a CPA and advisor, to prepare our next offering.

Chuck and Lina did the modeling. They included multiple scenarios: best and worst case, realistic and conservative. The model took into consideration the number of restaurants, the ramp-up to profit at each restaurant, leveraging of fixed corporate expense, and growth of corporate infrastructure expense along with the required revenue offset while still maintaining best-in-class margins. They laid in our current debt with different scenarios. The goal was to show what the company would look like over one, three, and five years.

We landed on $3 million as the amount we needed. Our preference was to find one investor to write one check for the full amount. After the previous small rounds, our capitalization table (investor roster) was already getting long.

This next round of financing would require that we start acting like a public company—beginning with more sophisticated, detailed record keeping. We would also need to have audited or at least reviewed financial statements done by a reputable accounting firm. If we were going to be put through a due diligence process with an investor, everything we were reporting and predicting had to stand up to scrutiny. We had to be able to confidently share a model with a five-year growth forecast that could handle the valuation we were proposing. We also had to get clear on the "cachet" or investor-perceived "secret sauce" of our brand. In addition, we had to understand the temperature of the market in our industry segment. Was it hot or not?

Founders will say, "This is what we think the valuation should be," but potential investors will have their own opinion. They will try to poke holes in your number. A strategic partner will say, "We can provide these things you're deficient in—it's not just about the money but also about services we can provide and savings we can help you achieve." Some of these might be intangible, like association with powerful people in their network. Other resources might be access to their general and administrative functions, technology, or marketing. Whatever they possess, they might use that to lower the valuation. They may also look to discount the valuation because of other perceived risks to their investment. This is often referred to as "the haircut."

This process of upscaling would kick off a period of massive learning for Lina and for us as partners. With a solid model and a deeper understanding of our negotiating points and deal breakers, we felt (metaphorically) like we were able to get out of our pajamas and dress like grownups. We assembled an offering with Frank's and others' help, then made a short list of people we wanted to talk to. We took numerous meetings to learn what investors' appetites were and to assess their tolerance for our proposed deal terms. Our presentation might go great, but then we'd get their paper offer and check it against our terms. Having that list in advance makes the process much cleaner.

One major lesson was that the big league investment guys don't want to write small checks. It doesn't, as they say, "move the needle" on their portfolios. Frank suggested a source of investment that was unfamiliar to us—family offices.

Frank knew from experience that family offices are guided by their own values and beliefs. Often a family office's mission is to grow capital for the family's long-term, multi-generational wealth planning. This approach fit with our ideas about sustainable practice and provided an attractive antidote to faceless corporate entities. Family offices offered an attractive bridge to large private equity. With the right family office, we were likely to find an investor willing to write smaller checks, be hands off, and possibly not require board representation.

Frank introduced us to Don Laden and the Mathile family office. Several meetings and some negotiations later, Organic Capital took the full $3 million offer. We had our one investor with one check.

RECOGNIZE THE INHERENT CONFLICTS OF INTEREST

When the deals get bigger, the number of people around the table increases too. Of course each one has a stake in the outcome; it's the way deal making works. But it's important to have your eyes open about whose best interests are being served.

We remember taking some meetings that didn't feel right, like the fox had been let into the henhouse, where we were treated less as equals than as opportunities. Walking into a boardroom with an enormous black granite table was not our vibe. We wanted to deal with respectful, high-integrity, reliable investors. Bob Franko was our banker; we were his client: that relationship was clear and dependable.

Once we moved into transactions with investment advisors, life got more complex. At one point, we pushed back on what was a generous offer because we had other potentially attractive options. In an effort to manage both sides of the deal, our investment banker said, "If you don't take these terms, you run the risk of losing the deal." He doesn't want to piss off the investor or alienate us, and of course he is mindful of his commission. It's a complicated relationship with inherent conflicts of interest. We tactfully turned down the offer. It was the right thing to do and eventually resulted in a deal we could accept.

EMOTIONS SHOULDN'T DRIVE YOUR DECISIONS OR YOUR VALUATION

Markets get hot and it's easy to get swept up in the money flow as investors rush in. We were students in a competitive industry. Once private equity discovered the fast casual niche, there were deals going down like crazy. We tried to learn from the hits and the misses.

At times that meant having to manage jealousy. Erik got a call from another entrepreneur after we had passed on an offer from private equity. The entrepreneur called to thank us for passing because he was next on their list. He did a deal with them, and suddenly he could afford a new house, a Rolex—those signs that you've *arrived*. At the time, the weight of founder's fatigue descended on us. It was natural to second-guess that we'd missed the boat, that those doing the deals were the smart ones while we stubbornly stuck to a plan that might not work out.

Over time, we watched many of these deals fail or at least not turn out as the founders had hoped. La Boulange and Umami Burger stand out as high-profile transactions that fizzled. We learned a lot from objectively observing and remaining patient.

It was hard not to be envious of The Counter Custom Burgers when they were chosen by Oprah as the best burger in the U.S. But what happened next was an unfortunate cautionary tale: they franchised like mad and it looked like they were losing control.

Meanwhile we saw successful tactics like Sweetgreen bolstering its brand credibility by touting all the famous New York chefs they had attracted as investors. We watched the strategies, the up-and-comers, and the flameouts as the fast casual sector became the object of lots of investment dollars looking for big, fast returns. We had to keep our head and not let other deals tempt us into inflating our valuation. We chose to stay the course we'd set for patient capital and values-aligned partners. It wasn't easy.

YOU CAN SAY "NO" WITHOUT LOCKING THE DOOR

One early temptation came in the form of being sought out by a private equity group. They discovered us around 2011 after we were well established in West Hollywood. The courtship started very soft touch with conversations like "we want to get to know you," "we can give you insights into the industry," and "you're the most exciting brand in the world." It wasn't until later we discovered that this is the same pitch all founders get to caress their ego.

That particular group of equity investors was already fairly deep in our industry segment and enjoyed a good reputation as an early stage investor. They had chosen their investments wisely and had done well. We hadn't heard a lot of negatives about them and they weren't the least bit aggressive. It made sense to start talking with one of the top restaurant investors.

The courtship meant many dates that finally led up to an offer. But before we saw the details there was a super expensive dinner with all the key equity players. We were wined and dined and everybody was in great spirits. After dinner, they gave us their paper. Let's just say we were glad we didn't have to pay for dinner, because it was not a deal we could or would do.

After we had time to consider their offer, we didn't cause a scene or go silent. Frank advised us to tell them we're thinking it through. The low valuation and amount of company control they were asking for were non-starters for us. We decided carefully how to answer. It worked because their response was, "We'd like to keep talking."

Sometime later they said, "We've done some soul searching and had some internal conversation. Historically, we would only take a controlling interest but we're open to a minority role. Where are you now?" Because we'd stayed on course to pursue patient money outside of private equity, we had access to people able to write bigger checks and bring quiet value. We could still politely decline.

Dealing with highly experienced equity players taught us to keep our eyes open. Know that savvy investment groups are always going to try to buy low and sell high. That's the deal. Don't be wooed by all the flattery that comes before the paper. Ultimately, private equity fund managers have limited partners to report to, who charge them with ensuring the predicted return on their investment. At the end of the day, it's a transaction, nothing more.

After that we closed the lines to private equity—we weren't taking any calls or meetings. We went dark, which only built-up demand. We were finding capital and support from trusted sources who were not intent on wresting control of Tender Greens.

Chapter 14

Knowing What Matters: Preparing for the Deal of the Decade

"No one else is going to build the life you want for you. No one else will even be able to completely understand it. The most amazing souls will show up to cheer you along the way, but this is your game. Make a pact to be in it with yourself for the long haul, as your own supportive friend at every step along the way."
— *Tara Mohr*

*W*e're getting noticed and people want to meet. How do we sort out the beneficial offers from the bad deals? How prepared are we to ask the scary questions that will reveal "strictly money" partners versus "strategic" partners? Our long-term goals—not fatigue or infatuation—had to drive the choice.

QUESTION THE THINGS THAT WILL MATTER NOW AND LATER

Each time we faced a significant decision as founders, we went back to our Ten Year Plan to level set. It's not that it held all the answers. But it did unmistakably state the values we had pledged to operate our business by. When we began again to field inquiries from private equity, we needed to make sure that everything we'd built would not be swept away by the power of outside money.

Doing an equity deal is first a financial decision. We'd spent the years and the effort to create a strong valuation. But for us, the deal also has to answer some larger, philosophical questions: Would I be proud to be part of this group? Can I stand in front of my team and announce we've sold a chunk of the company to X? Will their reaction be "that's amazing!" or will they fear that this will be the death of us?

The Tender Greens brand meant so much to us that we wouldn't do anything to compromise it. While the industry might celebrate a deal, we were concerned that our guests and team members could see it very differently. Customers only get half the story, and a whiff of a beloved neighborhood restaurant going "corporate" can cause people to abandon the brand. Our leadership team was made up of many who had been with us along much of the journey. Preserving their value after the deal was a genuine concern. All of these matters figured in our decision-making process. We attempted to describe the investor of our dreams before we started seriously shopping for one.

After developing a long list of questions, we started taking meetings with a small number of potential investors. We did our homework, checking out everything available, getting familiar with how the entities operated, and working with our investment banker to acquire more detail. This process helped us avoid wasting time talking with groups that seemed like a poor fit.

Below are some of the questions that evolved as we entered into discussions with Union Square Hospitality Group (USHG), with whom we eventually signed. We include a sampling here to show the categories that mattered most to us. Broadly speaking, we wanted specifics about expectations for operations and accounting, company culture, governance, competing interests, future plans, and potential conflicts.

- What are the expectations regarding the frequency and detail of reporting?

- What are the expectations regarding board meetings? Face-to-face? Teleconference? Frequency? New York or LA or both?

- What is the tenor of board meetings in their culture? Formalized? Roberts Rules? More informal but following a set agenda?

- What is the opinion on keeping our board to 5+1 as opposed to 7+1?

- What are the desires relative to how this story is told? What's to be discussed? What isn't? What can we share proactively with our team (at the appropriate time) so it feels respectful to our organization?

- What areas could be a conflict of interest? (An obvious one would be real estate.)

- Do you have a vision for our brand beyond the current plan?

- We had a great time getting to know the key players. Is there other energy (a "dark" side) we need to know about?

- What don't you want us to know about your organization?

Just shy of the ten-year mark, Tender Greens was a maturing successful brand. That doesn't mean we didn't have some resource gaps or areas in need of improvement.

Specifically, we thought the right strategic partner could bolster our marketing and branding, enhance our technological capabilities, provide deeper human resources to support mentorship and professional development, and possibly help with real estate and expansion. We'd been eyeing markets in states closer to California, but the East Coast was also attractive. The right partner could be a bridge to the East Coast, something that seemed too daunting for a California-based brand to execute alone.

BE HONEST. EXPECT HONESTY

Due diligence is central to this process. There's the standard stuff that happens—potential partners are looking at our financials, strategic plan, rate of growth, and projections. Meanwhile, we're wondering what we really know about these folks. It's only going to work if all sides are transparent and working toward building trust.

We were clear about our need to understand how potential partners act as an organization. The conversation starts with understanding what their expectations are for their investment. But it goes beyond measuring returns. What would you do if we miss the budget for a quarter? How do you resolve conflict? How do you deal with bad news? How do decisions get made in your organization?

By asking these sorts of questions, we were revealing who we were and what was important to us. Our culture, our approach to conflict, the way we treated our team and each other—we were completely candid about all of that. Being honest, and expecting honesty in return, helped us eliminate some equity suitors well before reaching the Letter of Intent stage. Our self-awareness meant we had to be philosophically aligned for a deal to work.

Before the team from the Cheesecake Factory showed up for a meeting, we were already thinking the deal wasn't right. In the process, however, we learned surprising, impressive things about their organization. Finally, it emerged in our talks that their chief motivation in acquiring Tender Greens was to quickly grow their top line revenues. Their valuation of our company was likely to be on the very conservative side. We passed.

Keith Pascal and Ron Shaich from Panera got further along in the process. We liked them a lot and frankly we knew we could learn from their technology, systems, and management of a complex supply chain. Ron generously spoke to our management team and it was inspiring to hear from such a successful founder. Much as we liked them, it was not the right brand fit. Erik summed up the opportunity, "It would have meant we were painting ourselves beige and moving to the suburbs." (Said with all due respect to those who love beige and the suburbs!) Panera was not an aspirational brand for us. They would have brought growth intelligence, but it was not the right fit.

It was disappointing each time a deal failed to materialize. We were still struggling, often feeling like we were trying to make it to Friday. It took us some time to realize that each founder should take a little money off the table when they can to give them breathing room—some space to focus on building the company and not constantly stress about making their rent. We came to realize that if we're resenting our own company because it's not affording us with financial happiness, we're likely to make the wrong decision when money comes calling.

The personal and professional stresses we all felt only show how important it is for founders to take care of themselves. The lights can go out and everything we've built is gone, through no fault of our own. Best to take care of our main resources—all the elements that make up a satisfying and sustainable life.

David introduced us to the Wheel of Life exercise. This is a tool you can use to assess where you are in the important functions of your life—what's your level of satisfaction right now toward family, wealth, health, friendships, fun, romance, spirituality, home, and personal growth? Too often, founders keep slogging toward some imagined future payoff when everything will be restored to balance. The Wheel of Life often reveals where there's little or no satisfaction and challenges us to figure out how to fix it. Can I hire someone part-time? Can I outsource? Can I quit working at 5 p.m. so I can have dinner with my kids?

Because we committed to a ten-year horizon and agreed that we would navigate the lean years together, we were better able to complete the marathon of building a business. This common bond helped us walk away from potentially bad deals and avoid other tempting offers for the first nine years.

Chapter 15

Two Closings: Business and Personal

Life is a song - sing it. Life is a game - play it. Life is
a challenge - meet it. Life is a dream - realize it. Life
is a sacrifice - offer it. Life is love - enjoy it.
– Sai Baba

IT'S A BUSINESS TRANSACTION

*I*t may sound strange but the process of selling significant equity
in Tender Greens ran a lot like traditional mating rituals. We let
it be known we were available. We went on some tentative dates
and depending on how these went, we began to narrow the field of
possibles. We looked for mutually positive signs from a prospec-
tive "match" before negotiations began.

We moved into dating mode in 2015, the ninth year of Tender
Greens, on schedule for our Ten Year Plan. By this point we had
twenty-two California locations with revenues of around $80
million.

We were big enough, solvent enough, and showed enough potential for continued growth to attract serious equity investment and
restaurant industry interest. We'd been fielding inquiries from
various parties, rejecting some right off as a bad fit, but looking

more seriously at several others. Despite our efforts to go into the process of bringing on an equity partner with our eyes fully open, we still had a blind spot. When Danny Meyer, a hero of ours, was mentioned, we were dazzled by the marquee name.

ASK THE SAME QUESTIONS OF EVERYBODY

Danny's stellar reputation was based on decades of successful brand building and hospitality operations. We were so focused on the prospect of working with Danny, Shake Shack and his USHG leadership team that we didn't stop to consider how forceful the private equity component would be. Private equity often uses this method, enlisting someone that founders respect as a way to open the conversation. It proved very effective with us.

On our list of perfect partner traits, Danny and USHG ticked off most of them. The Tender Greens culture had been built by food-driven people from the fine dining world. Danny Meyer was a name respected by our chefs. We could look forward to gaining some important things we were lacking—association with a fine dining pedigree, successful East Coast operations, real estate savvy, a more sophisticated growth plan like Shake Shack's, even potential international opportunities. This was a merger that would be celebrated in the industry and by our team that understood who Danny was and the excellence his company stood for.

With seven months of complex negotiations behind us, we closed the Series A round with USHG and the private equity firm Alliance Consumer Growth (ACG) taking a substantial minority position. Our longtime advisor, Frank Vizcarra, spoke the truth when he said, "The good news is you just got a big check. The bad news is you just got a big check."

This deal would provide us with the financial return we'd been working toward for the past decade. It also let us fulfill our promise to the original investors who signed on to our vision for Tender Greens—a liquidity event after ten years if we were successful. The benchmark for many equity investors is a return of 20x; we were able to surpass that ROI for those who believed in us from the early days. A lavish dinner was planned to celebrate reaching that milestone.

Just like a wedding, it was a bit overdone. We booked the entire chi SPACCA restaurant in LA for our group of sixteen or so. Chef/owner Nancy Silverton planned an impressive menu highlighting chi SPACCA's signature dishes, complemented by perfect wine selections. For this special meal involving sophisticated bankers, lawyers and a lot of money, it was all about big cabernets and tomahawk steaks—living up to the expectations of excess that many in business expect as a sign of achievement.

A champagne reception kicked off the evening. David was very good as host to keep things light and moving along. He graciously shared a personal anecdote related to each member seated at the table. The food was terrific as can be expected with Nancy Silverton behind the stoves. She's a legend in our business and a cook's cook.

Later that evening, when we sat for a photo with Danny and Nancy, we realized this was what we were so excited about. Yes, the personal wealth earned from the transaction transformed our lives overnight. But the career achievement of standing shoulder-to-shoulder with titans of our business was intoxicating. We were like kids finally getting to sit at the adult table. Heads spinning, we missed the powerful symbolism represented by the others in the room. Investment bankers, lawyers, private equity folks and key executives all had a hand in this deal. Now that it was done, they were already scouting for the next Tender Greens to acquire. The truth is, we didn't have a clue about how things were going to change.

STAY PRESENT

The next day, bleary eyed from wine and red meat, we resumed the business of Tender Greens. Only this phase would look and feel a lot different. What should have been joyful felt strangely un-emotional. We needed some time to absorb what had happened. It was unsettling not knowing what shape our roles might take. We knew we weren't interested in just going through the motions of being engaged. Not after working with such deep intention for so long.

Over the previous decade, David had been experimenting with plant medicine. He had always wanted Erik to join but the timing was never right. Spiritually stuck, Erik decided to join David in an Ayahuasca ceremony—based in the Peruvian tradition of spiritual healing.

At the Journey, we drank our tea and sat in quiet stillness. Within half an hour, joy began to seep in. Soon we were both in different worlds. It was relaxed and calming. Erik felt himself cradled in the arms of the Divine Mother—a sort of universal goddess. Her energy wrapped him in love—the sort of intense comfort only a mother can provide. All of the stress, worry, anxiety, fears of life stored up over the years began to release. What Erik felt was a profound message—"You're OK now. You've done well. I'm proud of you. Now you can rest."

That experience was like a fever breaking, a total spiritual release. An opening of great light let in a renewed sense of purpose. It was an invitation to re-engage. The Divine assured Erik, "You have what you need. Now, help others."

David's experience was similarly profound. In the ceremony he saw the form of a gentle, big-eyed cow. She had three hearts and they were Matt, Erik, and David. When Matt left, one heart stopped. The cow went through a transformation and was able to adjust to having only two hearts. Then Erik left. Another heart stopped beating. That sweet cow had to make do with one heart, and that was David. He felt deeply that this lovely cow, our company, needs one heart, even if it was an amalgam of the three of us represented only by David. He realized this was a prophecy and that he needed to pass on the role of "beating heart" to the next generation of Tender Greens leaders.

After the ceremony, we lay in the grass in Venice, California, looking up at the night sky. We hugged each other. At Tender Greens, we routinely did check-ins to see how each other was holding up and who needed help. We'd tell each other, "I'm at a 7.5 or an 8." After the Ayahuasca, we both checked in at "a powerful 10." We sat in that celebration—the personal, powerful, and restorative event we craved.

We share this experience for what it reveals about the way forward for founders. We had speculated about reaching our goal, but there's a big difference between understanding conceptually and being in it—finding how different it is emotionally.

We were about to learn why it's very difficult for founders to stay on long term. For an intense decade, we'd been in build mode. Our lives were all about mission and purpose. After the sale, the metrics for success changed.

Chapter 16

The Business Life Cycle: Growth Pains for Tender Greens

"Truth is you don't know what is going to happen tomorrow.
Life is a crazy ride, and nothing is guaranteed."
– Eminem

*W*ith perseverance, luck, and skill we'd grown our business to the defining pinnacle we'd set a decade or so before. But the business was only an adolescent. The next stage, early adulthood, was the next developmental challenge in terms of skills, experience, and vision. With new equity partners and new aspirations we encountered unforeseen stresses to the business and to us as founders.

NEW PARTNERS CHANGE THE POWER DYNAMICS

In hindsight, our intuition and comfort were strained between what we believed was right for the brand and our openness and desire to be good partners with our new investors. We had a blind spot about the role the equity partner would have in influencing marketing, branding, real estate, technology, and most painfully, key personnel. If we had asked those same assessment questions of ACG's Josh Goldin and USHG's Danny Meyer, the answers would have been very different. ACG has a different business model that is hugely successful, but we weren't considering that. When we should have been looking holistically at all the investors, we stayed focused on Danny as the one most familiar and known to us.

All our equity partners wanted to help us achieve what we talked about during due diligence—continued growth and success for the brand. We listened and accepted guidance even when it made us uncomfortable. We had to learn to trust Danny's wisdom and Josh's savvy, even when they put us outside our comfort zone.

In the short run, when we closed the deal with USHG and ACG, we felt great. We were concerned about being able to meet expectations for the future, but because of our past success we felt we should be able to hit the mark with our eyes closed. We signed the deal and delivered a healthy return to our legacy shareholders. That felt deeply gratifying.

But nothing is ever that simple. There were many consequences we had not anticipated.

As we think back on the aftermath of the liquidity event with USHG and ACG, a sports analogy best captures the feeling. It was like we'd had a commanding lead for most of the game. Then suddenly we're down in points. We're playing defense and the ball is not bouncing our way. We felt our confidence erode. It became more and more difficult to defend against the pressure.

The relationship with our new board started out agreeably enough. They were supportive in the first few months and we were delivering results. Taking action where they suggested, especially in areas where we knew we were vulnerable like marketing and branding. After years of learning from our advisory board, we felt we knew how to sort out good from less useful advice while staying true to our vision and values.

But with everyone's sights now set on growing to a $1billion company through rapid expansion, we found ourselves in a different league. In the ten years since Tender Greens opened its doors, a phenomenal number of new restaurants in our sector and in our neighborhoods sprang up. Competition for real estate, construction crews, and restaurant labor pushed up costs exponentially. On the marketing side, social media burst on the scene. Overnight, everybody was posting on Instagram. Food imagery became so common, it was harder and harder to cut through the noise—it was as if guests had developed attention deficits.

Previously, we would have responded to each of these increasing pressures iteratively. We had always problem solved that way: Try something on a limited scale. See if it worked. If yes, go bigger with it. If no, regroup and try another tactic. When our numbers started to soften a bit, the more vocal board members came up with more "suggestions." We were kind of "yeah, we got this" but in the board's view we weren't proactive enough.

We were trying to see the value in what these executives had already done. They knew bigger systems. They had already taken brands international. They had flourished through rebranding. We listened to hear what we could gain from their advice. Almost immediately, though, some things didn't feel right.

Throughout the growth of Tender Greens, the "three amigos" Matt, David, and Erik had led and made decisions as a stable three-legged stool. Yes, we had some wobbly times, but we were deeply committed to our partnership based on valuing what each of us brought to the business. The board didn't share that view. In their opinion, we were not being decisive enough and we didn't have the right senior leadership team in place.

Prior to the first meeting of the new board in New York City, we got a heads-up that a reorganization needed to happen. The three of us talked it through in advance and agreed to honor whatever the reshuffle looked like. Early indications led us to believe that Erik or David were under consideration as CEO. We were all OK with that and agreed we would still support one another.

At the meeting, the board made clear that they "only want one person at the top. It's important for the functioning of the company ... (we're) not going to call three of you when a decision has to be made." Erik stepped up for the job. As a result, he became the direct line to the most engaged board members, Danny Meyer from USHG and Josh Goldin from ACG.

From this meeting on, Erik's full-time job seemed to be about managing the volume of board-led "interventions"—notes, input, opinions, feedback. We had never previously experienced anything like this from the people involved in our business. Everyone was acting in good faith, but the messages weren't always clear or consistent from all parties.

These were major decisions like the target for geographic expansion. There was relentless pressure for us to enter New York City. We told the board we were excited to go east but couldn't pencil it out. Expanding into adjacent markets like Texas, Las Vegas, or Arizona offered growth potential that seemed to us more attainable and much less expensive. Struggles like these, and deep disagreement over the composition of our management team, burned cash and distracted us from blocking and tackling the intense competition we were facing in the marketplace. We were focused on the wrong things, expending energy that did not protect or advance the company when it needed that attention.

This intense board pressure was not wrong or ill-directed, but it created a dynamic that made it difficult for us to make the best decisions for the company. We simply weren't skilled at managing this new layer of oversight.

One source of tension that grew in intensity centered on Matt. With disappointing results in real estate and development—budget overruns, opening dates missed, questionable location choices, we asked the board for guidance. What other help might Matt need? What about our process needs to change? For a decade, we had almost obsessively tried to protect our leadership structure. Now trying to find the bridge between the board and our senior management was reminiscent of the stresses between the operations team and the home office staff in our earlier days. Both groups had different perspectives on what job needed to be done. We might have aligned outcomes, but the pathways diverged. Being at odds like that creates internal tensions. Trying to communicate with both sides and finding the right way forward is difficult, delicate work.

Faced with shrinking margins and the strains of high financial expectations, controversy over leadership was a troubling distraction and an emotional drain. It created a destructive wedge in our founders' partnership. The change in structure affected each of us differently. Erik became absorbed in translating the suggestions of the board into action. David settled into task mode by leading the executive team. Matt struggled to find his voice in the new order which eventually led to his early retirement. In retrospect, it's easier to see that by trying to bolster some of our team, we were kicking the can down the road.

BE OPEN TO ADVICE BUT DON'T ABANDON WHAT BUILT YOUR SUCCESS

We learned this the hard way by discounting our proven process and, at times, too uncritically accepting another way to lead. What had always worked for us was operating as a learning culture. We had done things iteratively—pull back and pivot, gain confidence and move ahead.

In this environment of heightened expectations—more potential for risk and reward—we faced so many areas of the unknown. For instance, the increasing dependency on sophisticated technology running through every cell of the company—from third-party delivery to social media to every level of the hospitality industry. Our board wanted speed and sophistication. That wasn't really who we were or how we had built the business.

For this next stage of growth, we went fast because we were being pressured to. And we pushed that pressure down through our management ranks. We went too fast with our existing team who had new, huge projects to deal with while simultaneously managing all their previous responsibilities. We hadn't fortified the team enough. We wanted the same people who had grown to their current level within the company to do much bigger things that were beyond their professional exposure and skill set.

When the board pressed us to go through a rebrand, our painful experience offers a good example of best intentions leading to unintended consequences.

The original Tender Greens logo was a homemade design. Erik's brother sketched a leaf. David downloaded the font. Period. It had a folksy, earthy tone to it, but the board said it was aging out. We needed something new. We recognized that Tender Greens was a more difficult thing to brand now because the landscape of fast casual was very crowded. We didn't want to get left behind in a sea of sameness. Or have a look that said to young people, "This is a place our parents go with their friends." Our brand was beginning to feel like Facebook, while newer brands were Instagram. The board recommended that we hire a prominent New York firm with recent success in the hospitality space.

For two days, we drove a representative of a prestigious New York design firm around to our LA stores and listened to them telling us how subpar our brand was. They also let us know that if what we wanted was a "refresh or a tweak" they were not interested. That should have been a red flag, indicating the project was more about the agency's creativity than it was about our brand or what we wanted. The design firm came back with three options. None of the options resonated with us, but the board encouraged us to choose. After all, this firm was in the design hall of fame and we weren't.

Our biggest concern centered on the rapid East Coast growth of the restaurant chain Sweetgreen. Our designer was surely familiar with that brand, but somehow came back with uncomfortably similar looks. Still we had to pick one, so we did. When he saw our new logo, Nathaniel Ru, one of Sweetgreen's founders, called us to ask what we were thinking. The way he saw it, instead of setting us apart, Ru said, "You're colliding with us." We had not had the courage and confidence to hold out for something unique, or at least better. We felt like a home run hitter who could no longer reach the fence.

Rebranding wasn't the only accelerated process. We were pushed to do multiple major changes at the same time—change our marketing, alter the menu and, crucially, hire high-level executives from the outside to help lead growth. It was all about entering the East Coast as a new brand, not the old brand. Revolution not evolution. As leaders we didn't have a good roadmap for this fast-paced journey. We were being driven by board pressure, unable to see the road ahead.

The rebrand was extreme. Expansion to the East Coast was extreme. And hiring from the outside to form a new executive team was even more extreme. We ended up spending a lot of time, money, and goodwill in the rebrand, bringing on VP or C-suite level executives from the outside and trying to integrate them into our culture. We were struggling to manage the thought tensions between new and old, and the vastly different worlds of New York and California.

For the first time, we met serious internal resistance with the Tender Greens team we had so carefully nurtured and brought along with us. We no longer had alignment with our executive team. People in the home office were crying. While the board was celebrating the changes, our legacy team leaders were asking, "What are you *doing* to us and the company?"

These massive changes caused us to lose focus on what was really important—our people, product, and guest experience. We struggled much more than we should have. We worked way harder than we needed to. We wish now we had had the wisdom to approach growth systematically, in stages.

THERE'S A DIFFERENCE BETWEEN A HARD AND A DIFFICULT DECISION

Among the many wise things Danny Meyer passed on to us is that as leaders we will constantly be faced with hard and difficult decisions. The sooner we learn to recognize the difference, the more effective our leadership will be.

A difficult decision is one that requires some informed but dispassionate outside advice. What makes the decision difficult is that the answer is not clear. One can argue both sides. One can take any of a number of possible paths. Rushing to make the difficult decision—not taking the time to deliberate and figure it out—reduces the chance of making the smartest choice.

By contrast, a hard decision is crystal clear, but it's going to hurt. And these choices most frequently involve our greatest resource, our people. Failure to make the hard decision in a timely way is more than a painful distraction; it can do serious damage to an organization's morale, reputation, and success.

Our roots at Tender Greens went deep into personal loyalty—to each other as founders, to our team members, suppliers, investors, and guests. We wanted our culture to be loyal and kind to a fault to everybody. We were good at second, third, fourth chances for chefs and staff—it was part of what created the love. We weren't impulsive leaders who thought that the best way to solve a problem was to fire people.

Danny offered an analogy to help us recognize this stage in the business life cycle—the tree and the bark. For a tree to grow, it must shed old bark and make space for new bark. At Tender Greens, we held on to some bark for too long. We were motivated by the desire to care for people and at least try to create elegant outcomes or exits.

Christina Wong was one of the most visible and painful examples of the consequences of trying to avoid the hard decision of separating from someone we felt close to. Christina had been our PR person forever, first as an agency team member, then as our in-house lead. While we may have been distrustful of the marketing industry in general, we trusted Christina completely. She thoroughly knew our brand and always was spot-on representing us. But the needs of our company had grown in response to intense competition and required another level of expertise. Erik's belief in Christina caused him to drag his feet. We were trying to provide support for her by hiring additional staff. The board called us on it, criticizing us for having two people doing the job of one instead of hiring a replacement with more marketing firepower.

At the same time, we had been pushed way outside of our comfort zone—none of us had managed a chief marketing officer or a chief real estate developer. In a rapidly changing market, we were concerned that anybody with industry seniority might be too conventional and old school. But someone younger would not have the requisite track record. We wanted someone who could take the ball and run, who thoroughly knew what to do.

Finding the next senior management team members was a series of difficult decisions. We brought somebody in who was very talented but stayed less than a year. We chose a seasoned executive who had worked for an international brand, thinking that person would need only to become familiar with our culture. We thought we'd found a self-starting fatherly figure but instead we got an institutionalized approach that lacked the energy our expansion required.

Some of what we learned through this painful phase was the importance of bringing new senior management in slowly and intentionally, always being mindful of the potential impact on our culture. Adding to the overhead by hiring more industry heavy hitters in marketing, real estate and facilities was necessary. What was hard to avoid were some very sad goodbyes and disappointments felt throughout the Tender Greens organization.

There were also some successes. To fill the critical VP of operations position, we finally recognized we were mistakenly looking for an outsider with rollout expertise in multiple brands. What mattered more was energy, the ability to grow professionally, and a deep commitment to our brand. We promoted Pete Balistreri as VP, where he once again delivered the string of successes that was his hallmark.

We don't regret the nurturing style on which we built Tender Greens. Our amazing team made it possible for the business to succeed. It says a lot about our culture that when someone was promoted to mid-level management, they were celebrated and rewarded with a Tiffany key chain engraved with the message, "D.F.I.U.♥"—a secret loving code for "Don't fuck it up!"

Since then we have learned a hard truth—either your team members are growing to the next level, or it's time for them to move on. Our experience has shown us that it's often easier for an informed "outsider" to see this because they don't have emotional ties to individuals. We needed help to cut through the emotion and look critically at our team, asking two essential questions: Can they do the job? Will they do the job? Then we needed support to make decisions based on this honest assessment.

It's inevitable that there will be a "tree and bark" crisis as your company grows. Most likely, personnel mistakes will be made that are costly in more ways than money. Still, these are essential, valuable, important decisions. Making those hard decisions in a timely manner is key. But so is taking the necessary time to make the right new choices so it doesn't shift the culture too dramatically at the top.

It feels like we moved too quickly on some of those issues. Yet the board would say we were too slow. The impact of so much management turmoil soon affected each of us deeply.

Chapter 17

Changes at the Top: Handing over the Keys

"When I stand before God at the end of my life, I would hope that I would not have a single bit of talent left, and could say, I used everything you gave me.
– *Erma Bombeck*

*A*s social entrepreneurs, we built our business in a personal way to "do good while doing well." We had attracted the team and the investment that fueled the next stage of growth while preserving the DNA of the company. With higher stakes and expectations, we could sense a shift in priorities and accountability. We began to feel that something was not quite right. It was time for us to evaluate what was best for us and for our company.

FOUNDERS AND BUSINESSES HAVE LIFE CYCLES

During 2016-17, we were trying to settle into the first wave of board-driven reorganization. Erik was CEO, David was president, Matt was VP of real estate. We thought it would be smart to share the leadership along defined lines. Erik had marketing but given our ambitious growth plans, he would also support Matt. David had operations, HR, and finance. We tried that on for a while, but in retrospect, this structure did not play to our respective strengths. When the company started to struggle, the board suggested that we professionalize the leadership team by bringing in someone with more experience to lead the company forward.

In 2002 when we imagined completing our Ten Year Plan, we assumed we'd find our own replacements. We thought we'd outgrow executive roles at Tender Greens. We'd each be ready to move on to the next thing. What we didn't want was to find ourselves stuck, like an athlete past his prime who can't seem to retire. Or shuffled into a stream of new titles, each more meaningless and marginal than the last, until finally being sidelined altogether.

So when the board brought up the idea of bringing in a new president, we didn't disagree. We met with Josh and Danny to formulate a plan. After a few months of letting the idea sit, we activated a search.

As CEO and current president, Erik and David led the search. We started with some strong preferences for the sort of person we hoped to find and with a commitment to diversifying our leadership. Denyelle Bruno easily stood out from a crowded field.

Denyelle was LA-based, a Tender Greens guest, and many things we admired: a mom, a smoker of clove cigarettes, adept at karaoke Elton John performances. Seriously, she was deeply skilled but also anti-corporate. We could sense how readily she would be accepted and respected by our chefs and managers.

Her professional experience was varied and rich. The time she spent at Macy's West mirrored our stints in the conservative, guest-oriented hotel business. She'd been at Apple during Steve Jobs's leadership and had been part of the creative disruption caused by the rollout of Apple retail stores. At Peet's Coffee, she helped this OG of premium coffee—a folksy, Berkeley-born hippie brand—grow to maturity while retaining its special, unique qualities. Moving to Drybar, Denyelle knew what it was like to manage a first mover with a slick, modern, fast-moving brand.

Denyelle didn't come out of the restaurant business, but all her previous roles enabled her to understand our guests. The woman who gets her hair blown out at Drybar is also a Tender Greens guest. Denyelle had been on both sides of industry shifts. She knew what it was to be the disruptor and the disrupted. We believed she had tools in her kit that we didn't have. Time has proven that to be true. She's a quick learner, able to make complex decisions with confidence drawn from rich past experience. Welcoming Denyelle to the Tender Greens family was a key strategic move at the right time.

With Denyelle on board, we were beginning to see some successes once again. But the wins did not feel personally energizing.

FOUNDERS CAN GET LOST. LISTEN TO YOUR INNER VOICE (PART 2)

In 2018, in order to help bring Tender Greens to the East Coast, Erik moved to New York City. He was already drifting away from the day-to-day concerns of the business. He felt that as the new executive team settled into their roles, his job had shifted to managing board expectations for growth.

Meanwhile, his heart and spirit were in leveraging Tender Greens' platform to further some of the things that were important to him—issues that had initially put him on the entrepreneur's path. He thought there was opportunity, for example, to position Tender Greens as a provider of nutrition to collegiate and professional athletes; to drive the issue of food as wellness to a larger audience; to go deeper into regenerative agriculture and biodiversity; to push the Tender Greens supply chain further in support of pressing food-system issues—i.e., going well beyond where other fast casual brands were willing or able to go.

He saw this as a point of valuable differentiation and business opportunity. While many brands claimed to support local food systems, Tender Greens had built its business on local and sustainable sourcing. Going even deeper as the company grew might help cancel some of the competitive noise in the fast casual space. The initiatives he was proposing might also open up novel revenue streams by targeting new audiences such as athletes.

These passions and the work he had begun doing with the Crop Trust, Rodale Institute, and Google Food Labs sent him down "a rabbit hole of beliefs and passion that created a delta or disconnect about the food system I imagined and the pressures to protect margins—whether it was labor or volume or supply chain." Fighting against a lot of internal pushback around the elite athlete pathway, for example, sapped some of his energy, though it later turned out to be a profit center.

His passion for biodiversity initiatives and regenerative agriculture went too far for the company to follow. While the Tender Greens chefs understood the importance of these concerns, they were preoccupied trying to control their food costs, budgets, and margins. Erik's need to innovate and reshape the food system—especially through regenerative agriculture, food equity, and food justice—was no longer satisfied by the ongoing demands of overseeing Tender Greens expansion.

At first, the move to New York was interesting. Opening one store in a new market was almost like going back to the start of Tender Greens. But being thousands of miles from our home office soon felt like being alone on the ground in unfamiliar territory without air support. The remote nature of the work made more pronounced the disconnect Erik had begun to feel even before leaving California.

"My values and interests were leading me away. It was less about being bored than about seeing a new team in place with new priorities driving the business. That's when I felt it was time for me to complete my work by grounding Denyelle in the intricacies of the food business and the Tender Greens value system. I wanted an orderly transition so I could feel satisfied to hand her the keys and phase out. I did not want to linger as a burnt-out, disillusioned, and dysfunctional leader."

By 2018, Matt Lyman had separated from the company. The loss of Matt created space for new talent but left an emotional hole for many of us. With the partnership splintering, David was feeling increasingly isolated. It was a difficult time.

From David's West Coast perspective, Erik was living the life in New York. Denyelle had taken on the challenges of navigating increased competition, a changed market, and an underperforming New York expansion. She had a relatively new team of outside hires as senior executives in marketing and real estate. Through internal promotions, some long-time Tender Greens staff took on new or expanded roles. First, Lina O'Connor assumed a richly deserved leadership role as CFO. Next came recognition to Pete Balistreri as VP of operations, and Matt Candito as director of operations. Together with Sam Innes, Christina Rodriguez, Lacy Moody and others, this next gen was the new "beating heart" of Tender Greens.

Although he was becoming dispirited, David still wanted what was best for the company. What appealed to him most was nourishing the Tender Greens culture—investing time and energy into teaching, training and the growth of people. It seemed, however, that this was something no one really had time for. Denyelle had often expressed that she could never have done what Matt, Erik and David had done to build the company. Yet it was clearly her responsibility to move the company forward.

David remembers what it felt like. "This new person who I really liked and admired came into our brand. I gave her my office! Suddenly closed door meetings were happening and I wasn't invited. Sadly, with the departure of our VP of people services, my position became an HR functionary role that I wasn't trained in and had no passion for, so I started to drift."

It was Denyelle who told him, "You're so much more than this job you're doing. Why are you doing it?" That got David in touch with his Capricorn sense of responsibility. His focus became making sure everyone, himself included, and the organization were going to be OK post-transition. It was the wrong time to bring in an HR VP, a move that would generate additional expense and internal disruption, so Denyelle and David agreed that he would stay for a year. During that time he was talking to Erik monthly and starting to feel aspirational for a next chapter. David recalls "feeling grateful Denyelle had given me permission that I hadn't been able to give myself."

Chapter 18

A Door Opens: Reinvention and Regeneration

"When, at last, I ceased to be myself, I came to be."
–Kamand Kojouri

M *ore than a decade ago we had a dream; although it was very real to us, it only existed in the vague realm of possibility. After ten years of intense engagement and, let's face it, considerable personal sacrifice, we made that dream real. Although our Ten Year Plan had an endpoint, we had been open to the idea of staying on with Tender Greens. Instead, after a while, exiting seemed the only real option.*

Leaving the business we built was never meant to be the end of our contribution to the world. Re-engaging with what interests us, with what we love, started us on our next journey. For most founders—including us—such a transition is inherently painful. But joy and new purpose greeted us on the other side.

MAKE IT YOUR DECISION

Our original concept for Tender Greens was to design a multi-unit brand that did not tie us to the daily operations forever. We had all worked for very talented people whose name was on the marquee;

they were expected to be working in the company as long as their name was on the sign. There were also entrepreneurs we admired like Wolfgang Puck and Joachim Splichal who avoided that trap. By making the business not about them but about what their respective brands, Spago and Patina, represented, and by elevating and celebrating others in their organization, they worked *on* the business, not *in* the business. Our Ten Year Plan for Tender Greens recognized that we wanted to build a brand that had lasting value beyond the involvement of the three of us.

Our original plan was clear—ten years to earn a payback on investment. As we concluded the T.Y.P. and set out on the next phase of growth, we were all in. We were excited to grow as a brand and as leaders. But as time went on one by one we lost momentum. We significantly underestimated the pressure of responding to supervision. We finally had the first financial comfort of our working lives. We had won the championship as it were, so we enjoyed the success and achievement, but staying meant having new bosses. That changed the dynamics for us as entrepreneurs.

Once the initial dramatic changes had started to settle at Tender Greens, Erik began to feel he was losing air. Going through a divorce, moving solo to New York, and feeling disconnected from his LA base proved to be too much. The new initiatives Erik hoped Tender Greens would pursue were continuously faced with resistance from the new management team. The compounding effect of all these factors was to disconnect him further. The combined factors accelerated his decision to leave.

Back in California, David sensed that Erik was already in a grieving stage about leaving Tender Greens. Erik felt bad about his decision to jump off the cliff, leaving David as the last man standing. But self-preservation and reinvention had to be the direction he chose. Every day he asked himself, "Am I turning away from everything?" There was an internal voice saying, "You need to push through this." But his heart was moving him in a different direction. There was guilt mixed in, not just about stranding David, but the people Erik cared about in the organization. There didn't seem to be any other way. He quietly went about a phased distancing.

David faced his own dilemmas. His long, close relationship with Erik became awkward even before Erik left for NYC. To David, it felt like his long-time partner had already jumped ship. There was a feeling Erik had gone rogue. David was trying to keep the peace with senior management, but honestly he felt deserted. It came down to a hard conversation. David asked Erik to be frank about what he wanted to do, because as things stood, it was not working for anyone.

As we prepared to step aside, we worked to leave behind a high-functioning organization. Now that the new senior management team was in place, we promoted Denyelle to CEO. Erik moved from CEO to executive chairman, acknowledging Denyelle's leadership while enabling a more discreet departure.

"That was a weird time between us," David recalls. "Then nearly a year later, when I was going through a similar time of unhappiness and doubt, we were talking monthly to commiserate. Just as it had for Erik, it became more and more obvious to me that I wasn't going to carve out a place at Tender Greens that worked for me." He realized the moment had arrived for him to jump off. He hoped that by separating from Tender Greens he would experience a bit of freedom and perspective and find new passion and purpose.

The best we could do was to be realistic and honest about the process. An exit is an exit. What we experienced was that we couldn't have it both ways—take the payout and somehow stay relevant and involved. We thought we'd be able to play important roles in the next phase of growth. Maybe if we had followed our path to more regional expansion into Texas, Arizona, and Vegas, things would have played out differently.

Everything we had laid out was happening, including our own sunset. Even though we had anticipated this, it was really hard. We think of this phase as "founders' empty nest syndrome"—you raise a child to go out and do great things and develop their own point of view. After they leave the house, you might discover their point of view doesn't seem to align as much with yours. They don't come home to visit. They hardly ever call. It's so hard to accept that this part of your identity is changing or fading. You can't dismiss the impact it will have on all aspects of your life.

Being able to leave the company you built on your own terms is a complicated challenge. It starts with giving yourself permission—asking yourself, "Haven't I earned a next step?" We were both a bit tired. And for some time it had ceased to be fun. It took a while to see, but that's not failure; it's an indication that we had evolved as founders.

Michael Mack, one of our advisory board members, shared with us what happened after leaving the company he built, Souplantation. "I took eighteen months off. I was bored, I was listless and my golf game wasn't any better." We didn't want that to be our future. While it wasn't at all clear what was next, we knew it was time to go. Better for the business, better for us personally and professionally. Maybe not a difficult decision, but a hard one.

ALLOW YOURSELF TIME AND SPACE

"Celebratory. Joyful. Easier." This is how Erik thought life would feel once he exited Tender Greens. Instead, the feelings that enveloped him were negative—"Anticlimactic. Liberating but lonely. Uncertain. Disconnected. Dishonest." It was a time of experiencing loss and of being lost.

After his exit, David could relate to these emotions, even though he had not suffered as many life changes as Erik had with divorce and a move cross-country. Still it felt like suddenly finding himself in a liminal state. Or as David describes it, "Having my ass between two chairs. I left the first chair, but I'm still trying to get comfortable with the second one."

Truthfully, we both experienced some dark nights of the soul. Disconnected from our titles and business, we began to feel like impostors. We forgot our success. We lost sight of the plain fact that we had done something remarkable. This form of depression colored our perceptions of everything we had accomplished. It made us ask, "How am I ever going to do anything else that will be this special?"

There are some practices that we both found helpful. One exercise is to write the "novel of your life." In short, you divide your life into equal segments, for example the years from birth to age 8, then from age 9-17 would be two early "chapters." And without getting mired in the details, you jot down the formative events or impressions you can recall.

Using this framework, we each worked through all our "chapters" up to and including the present. We listed in bullet form what we each had done in our lives that was special—adding which things were meaningful in our personal lives, our work lives, even in our education.

Using this information helped both of us remember our superpowers, gifts, and purpose. It helped us get a sense of who we might be able to help or what problems we might be able to solve in our next life iteration. We now use this tool as part of our coaching and advising practices to help entrepreneurs regain their sense of self.

We were fortunate to have colleagues and friends giving us feedback on what we had given them—saved some marriages, helped some careers, provided support when it was needed, created meaningful opportunity, and showed up as a true friend. Getting this feedback helped fill us up when our own identities seemed empty.

This reflective work revealed some options that could be even more rewarding than our work in the restaurant business. What if we could help people get unstuck, create and scale meaningful, purpose-driven businesses, be better leaders, have deeper relationships, and raise happier kids? Happier at work is happier at home and happier at home is happier at work. That seemed genuinely exciting.

We had each other to remind ourselves what we were good at. We knew each other's passions. We could encourage each other to explore those and think about taking on things we had wanted to do at Tender Greens that proved untenable.

For Erik, this uncomfortable period went on for nearly two years. During that time, he dove headfirst into a new, more supportive relationship. He returned to tried-and-true tools of self-care— daily meditation, fitness, great food, family, and a renewed purpose centered on regenerative systems. After dropping off the radar for a bit, he reconnected with friends. He lived as much in the moment as he could with no responsibility or commitments long term. "For the first time in my life," he recalled, "I couldn't see the future. I became OK with that state for a while."

In February 2020, before launching an advisory practice, David planned to take a week off to build a treehouse for his daughter's birthday. That was just before the pandemic began to shut things done globally. The pandemic gave him the gift of more time—to slow down and focus on family.

"There was some feeling of listlessness," David said, "but I didn't feel my entire identity was so wrapped up in Tender Greens that I didn't know who I was. The gap was that I didn't have a mission, or my mission hadn't started yet. I was used to being engaged with work that was all encompassing. Any new endeavor would have to enable me to do the things I loved most—to teach, inspire, engage in deep spiritual practice. The stuff I would have liked to extend and deepen at Tender Greens if the situation had been different."

While he was impatient to get rolling, the pandemic gave David a once-in-a-lifetime chance. He could spend time with his wife and kids in a way that never would have happened had he still been an executive in the COVID-embattled restaurant business. While he still wrestled with some guilt and shame about leaving Tender Greens, he was deeply grateful for his fortunate circumstances.

What we found, and other founders can corroborate, is how important it is to take your time before making new commitments. Relax a bit. Do a passion project first or a side hustle. Try things out—maybe the very things you neglected while you were so busy building your business. Pay attention to those. If your career was a nine on your Wheel of Life but your health or family satisfaction level was a six, you might ask yourself, "In this time when I have money in the bank, how do I take advantage of this opportunity to rebalance my Wheel of Life?"

DON'T DIVE IN THE DEEP END. RECONNECT

We are fortunate to be finding a way forward that is exciting and rewarding. But it's worth noting that both of us, all along this journey leading up to the conclusion of our Ten Year Plan, consciously and conscientiously worked to maintain a steady track of learning.

We came to value and rely on a strong network of mentors and trusted guides. Through these relationships at each turning point in the business, we were better able to deepen our skills and deepen ourselves. We embraced a practice of continuous learning and improvement. It benefited the business, but it also meant that when we arrived at the end of this body of work, we were better able to find a solid next step.

We benefited greatly with the help we received from so many generous people. And we are grateful we chose to dedicate the time and energy required to grow. The effort enabled us to show up with a set of tools that are useful to us and very possibly to others. It seems clear to us now that if you want to continue a full life of purpose, your preparation starts a lot earlier than the weeks or months leading up to your exit.

As founders, we are in a unique position for having done what we did. When you've lived in it for so long, your accomplishments seem less remarkable because it was your life. But when you look outside and listen to everybody's external perspective, you can begin to see that it *is* remarkable.

Once we genuinely accepted that we had done something few people do, in an industry that even fewer people do it in, we could see some future value. We could strive to become one of the aspirational models for a new generation of entrepreneurs. Over a decade ago, we had looked to those who went ahead of us for inspiration and information. Now, perhaps, it would be our turn to pay it forward.

Although we have left the day-to-day of Tender Greens, the team and relationships we enjoyed there remain part of our lives. In the beginning it was awkward. The last thing we wanted was to make anyone feel we were reaching out for gossip. David would send out an occasional "happy birthday" or other milestone message. Just a simple wish, not asking for anything or trying to hang on. Giving space was good for them and also good for us.

That's part of the healing process we've experienced. We're both personally at peace with it all. That acceptance affords us the line back to everybody with an open heart. And makes moving forward a journey without extra baggage.

Chapter 19

Not Our Last Words: Tender Greens and More, Post-Pandemic

"Do not dwell on the past, do not dream of the future, concentrate on the present moment."
– *Buddha*

As we considered our next life chapter, we recognized how much the restaurant business has changed since we launched Tender Greens in 2006. A recession, the exponential growth of social media, major shifts in consumer preferences, the ascendance of online ordering and third party delivery systems, and the most recent devastation caused by the COVID-19 pandemic combined to reshape this industry.

Tender Greens was not immune. Our East Coast restaurants closed in 2020 and those restaurants primarily in downtown/financial districts were temporarily shuttered as formerly bustling company offices remained empty. The painful furloughing of hundreds of team members was an inevitable consequence. The operations teams faced an urgent need to innovate, at scale, with far fewer staff and plummeting revenues.

Their creative, flexible responses led to a series of innovations in our restaurants---engaging our robust supply chain partners to create produce and grocery baskets, then kitchen and home essentials baskets, and as the pandemic stretched on, baskets to "create togetherness" featuring foods for sharing and making together (wine, cheese and charcuterie, barbecue and baking kits).

The Home Office staff, working remotely, did what they do best---supporting the restaurants by caring for team members, ratcheting back spending, and negotiating lease terms with landlords.

As founders we are proud of how the Tender Greens team, through unprecedented crisis, proved up to the challenge of innovating while protecting and enhancing the company culture. One testament to the enduring core of the organization is that, as the company recovers, furloughed employees are returning at every level of the organization. This is still the best job they ever had!

With the business stabilized and trending back towards pre-pandemic levels, Tender Greens saw an opportunity to share strengths and efficiencies through a merger. Tocaya and Tender Greens recently merged to form One Table Hospitality Group. The brands will continue to operate independently under leadership by a new senior management team that combines the expertise of each entity. Tender Greens brings depth in culinary talent and supply chain dedication; Tocaya's design and marketing strengths will certainly influence Tender Greens. Together the two brands are well positioned to lead California's fresh casual restaurant sector well into the future.

Our heartfelt congratulations to Lina O'Connor who features so prominently in this book as a key architect of Tender Greens. Lina now heads the leadership team for both brands. With all the complexity she and the One Table team face in merging the two companies and the on-going recovery, listening to her speak about the essential importance of the company culture is absolutely one of the most gratifying parts of this journey for us. We continue to play a role in the ongoing success of our beloved brand--Erik as a board member of One Table and David as a close mentor to Lina O'Connor as she carries the culture forward.

Inspired by the resilience of Tender Greens, we remain deep believers in the power of hospitality. Over the entire history of humankind, food has brought people together in ways that nothing else can.

Although we chose not to build a next business that required brick and mortar and the investment of lots of people and capital, we are all in when it comes to supporting the next generation of restaurateurs, food entrepreneurs, and everyone along their supply chain.

We believe in a bright future for reimagined hospitality. The role we envision for ourselves is best defined by Chip Conley, whose work and thoughts we admire. Chip describes moving from "the sage on the stage to the guide on the side." That's where we feel we can add the most value.

LET'S HEAR FIRST FROM ERIK

Following my separation from Tender Greens, I became an observer and a student. I tried to put myself in situations that allowed me to listen to the universe, whatever shape that takes. I believe the universe will make a suggestion, signal to you what it wants you to do. Either you accept that challenge or you don't. I listened to what was being asked or where I was being invited, then checked in with myself and my gut. If it was churning with excitement, that told me something. If I was listless, that sent another message.

My passions led me to food- and agriculture-centered organizations like Google Food Lab, the Crop Trust, and Rodale Institute. Initially, joining these organizations made it very easy to slip into impostor crisis mode. You're in a room where everybody seems more impressive than you. The questions in your head are, "How did I get here? Where can I contribute?"

For me, it came back to my core chef identity. I was almost exclusively the only chef at the table. These groups were looking to me to represent the chef community. To translate their moonshot plans into the language and the ecosystem chefs would relate to. To use my voice and platform as a successful member of the chef community to advance these ideas. Once I understood and accepted that, it gave me reason to step back into my chef identity. That's where I feel most comfortable anyway. Through that identity I am able to translate the policies and vision and ideas into the language of food.

Once I reconnected with my superpower, it gave me a focused lane I could own. I went through the exercise of identifying key search words for myself. In the process, it put me into proximity with chefs and influential food policy people I admire—people like Dan Barber and Alice Waters. The next level of introspection was asking, "How do I differentiate myself from them given that I can't compete on their level?"

Bolstered by the credibility of Tender Greens' success, I could advocate for the same ideals as Alice and Dan, but at scale and with broader access. That became my ownable lane. It ties me to my Tender Greens identity. It brings me back to our original premise, *good food for everybody.*

One expression of new opportunity is my connection to Cohere, a branding and marketing firm founded by my life partner, Antoinette Marie Johnson. Sharing my more seasoned experience with a new generation of young Cohere staff—with energy and language optimized for the times—gives me a sense of value.

Personally, I also enjoy serving as Antoinette's "guide on the side." When we first met, it struck me that I was the "plus 1" at the public event—she was the main attraction. In my past, I was accustomed to being the one in the spotlight. I knew exactly what Antoinette needed from me as her plus 1. This awareness of when to support and when to take the lead has made for a very powerful partnership. I often joke that she and I work similarly to how David and I worked: sometimes frustrating one another, but mostly getting it right.

With Cohere as a base camp, I have the space to explore my options from a foundation of food and the identity of chef. The universe was asking me to do two things: encourage entrepreneurs and speak out in favor of a healthier food system.

As an entrepreneur and now coach/advisor, I can help those who hope to travel a path similar to Tender Greens by sharing with them the framework and learnings of the Ten Year Plan approach. That desire led me to this book project.

And through the platform of Cohere, I can use my voice to advocate for Regenerative Food Systems. I leaned into the work of Rodale, Crop Trust, and Food Tank. This will likely be the topic of my next book and the focus of my cooking and farm practices. I will miss from time to time the good things about running a restaurant. But I have a greater desire to host highly curated experiences that are on my terms. I'll feed this desire with occasional events at the farm we are creating in Princeton or at the Viaduct event space we operate in Philadelphia.

To learn more or get involved follow @erikoberholtzer and Coherefoodlab.com

AND NOW FROM DAVID

As I was wrapping up my day-to-day responsibilities at Tender Greens, I decided to go back to school, completing a year-long coaching certification as well as a deeper dive in positive psychology. For this next chapter, I wanted to use my acquired wisdom, skills, and creativity to be of service to people. I knew I didn't want to launch into another complex project. I had collected a lot of great insights from our successes and failures at Tender Greens, from my personal work both with my wife and on my own, years of shamanic exploration with plant medicine, my involvement with a men's mentoring organization, and my study of spiritual psychology. I wanted to tune into a different and more holistic professional frequency.

In business leadership, it can be easy to dismiss anything not on the mind level of daily work as new age-y and overly ethereal. But I believe there's abundant value in what we can't easily see, like intuition or inner wisdom. Tuning into that allows us to hear our own thoughts and feelings differently and more deeply. There's really good information to be gathered there. The work is in getting people to slow down enough to hear it. If you want to have it shown to you, you have to ask for it. Our early years at Tender Greens showed me that. We'd built a culture on an intangible asset, love. In my next adventure, I wanted to pay that forward.

When I think back to what I loved most about building Tender Greens, it was going for a walk with a manager or sitting with one of the executives, listening intently and asking what I hoped would be helpful questions to support them to discover their own inherent wisdom about the challenges they were facing. And beautifully, more often than not, the conversation evolved from the original people or project issue to the deeper process work underneath—defining personal values and getting to the heart of what was probably impacting them in more places than just work. I fell in love with coaching.

As a student in coach training workshops, I noticed that many of my fellow participants were mid-level managers from different industries. Like me, they were looking to transition to a more fulfilling career. However, few had founded or scaled a substantial business. As a result, I had experiences and language that they didn't.

I had my own level of impostor syndrome when comparing myself to my gifted instructors and others like Marshall Goldsmith, Jerry Colonna, and Chip Conley whose work I was reading. Nonetheless, I could see that I had gifts that could be of service to founders and business executives. Not just as heart-centered business leaders but as human beings wanting to have more meaningful multi-faceted lives. The more I coached, the more I realized this need was not limited to my sisters and brothers in the restaurant business. My skills were transferable across industries.

My work as a coach is hugely rewarding. I serve as a quiet advisor to founders and executives to help them break down the ever-increasing complexities of business and life, speak directly and honestly about what I perceive, and, more than anything, remind them of their own strength and wisdom. I also happily jump in with teams to bring them tools to lead more powerfully, plan more effectively, and execute from a more heart-centered place. This work has brought me back to the thing that matters most to me: being of service.

For more information on working with David or to get in touch, please visit quietadvisory.com or follow @davidtdressler

CLOSING REFLECTIONS

Collaborating on this book project has given us a chance to re-live our formative experiences but also to revive our partnership. We've embarked on a joint venture of coaching, advising and mentoring, called simply TYP, that takes advantage of our left brain/right brain synergy in service to others—Erik's focus on enterprise and David's on leadership and soft skills. The prospect of creating a meaningful new business built on so many years of partnership and friendship is awesome.

It almost feels like the old days when we were sitting outside Shutters on the Beach or sipping the drip coffee we could barely afford at our "World HQ" Peet's Coffee in Santa Monica. We were deep in our plans and dreams for Tender Greens when everything was a possibility.

In our next iteration, we will continue to lean on our respective skill sets and the things we love to do. We have a chance for a second act together and that feels amazing.

ACKNOWLEDGMENTS

*W*e've told our Tender Greens story as we remember it, always mindful that without the talent, energy, and dedication of our team members there would not be a Tender Greens today.

To all the executive chefs, restaurant managers, home office folks, and every one of our amazing team members who built the business one delicious plate and one happy guest at a time, we are forever grateful. We thank your families too for sharing you with us. More specifically:

Adam Bussell for training new teams; Andrew DeGroot for setting new disciplines; Chris Kenney for bringing the fun, humor and culture to those in your light; Christina Wong for telling the story better than anybody; Cristina Rodriguez, Celeste Capaldo-Smith and Lani Sheridan for herding the cats; Cynthia Izaguirre Yilmaz for holding us accountable; Dan Robbins for refining our supply chain for national growth; Daniel Schaffhauser for truly honoring the title "chef"; Denyelle Bruno for making the tough choices we couldn't; Elderoy Arendse for his embodiment of the Tender Greens culture; Fermin Arias for working tirelessly in service of the mission; Lacy Moody for always doing it right; Lina O'Connor for believing in us and for carrying so much; Matt Candito for calmly rising to the company's needs; Michael Antoci for supporting our supply chain along the journey; Pete Balistreri for inspired leadership and dedication to special; Peter Balistreri for taking on NYC; Priscilla Lopez for showing us what determination looks like; Rian Brandenburg for putting his heart and soul into it; Sam Ennis for growing up with us; Scarlett Lindemann for being the first to get it, live it and grow it; Sean Canavan for growing the Bay Area.

A supportive community of growers, suppliers and service providers delivered the "good stuff" we set out to make more accessible and affordable. They made it possible for millions to experience how flavorful, comfortable and stylish healthy eating can be. Among them are:

Alex Weiser for growing the rainbow; Daniel Nollinger for believing from the beginning; George Yuen for supply chain strategy; Jason Buehler for making us tech smart; Mark Blancarte for the many locations; Mark Tepper for all the kitchens; Niccolo Valerio for elevated design; Paul Reeb for his dedication to organic farming and circular economies; the Stein Family for growing a supply chain with integrity; Steve Gabriel for teaching us how to be good partners.

Many individuals gave us the resources and encouragement to pursue our Ten Year Plan. We could not have succeeded without all that they generously brought to our endeavor. We especially want to thank:

Amin Ajani for working the floor at every opening; Andy Skov for his wisdom, vocabulary and thoughts on fatherhood over a waffle breakfast; Antoinette Johnson for your loving support and dedication to best in class; Barbara George Vandeman for pulling Base Camp Principles out of our hearts and heads; Bert Vivian for his calm, thoughtful voice; Bob Franko for caring enough to open his office and white board and for being a teacher; Cary Dressler for showing me "mensch"; Chuck Stevens for mentoring us in ways big and small; Danny Meyer for the elegant way he shows up; David Oberholtzer for the original logo; Demitri Hollevoet for his constant support and friendship; Don Laden for his patient and calming presence; Drew Oberholtzer for support when we needed it most; Eden Tull for bringing mindfulness to our team; Frank Vizcarra for more than we can say; Jeff Flug for challenging us with smart questions; Jenny and Spencer Figueroa for bearing witness and for naming the other man; Joachim Splichal for being a role model for us; Joel Weinstein for his wise counsel and friendship; Joseph Collins for believing in SLP; Josh Goldin for the tenacity to win; Karen Naylor for being an enthusiastic early reader; Kristen Irving for helping to shape the Sustainable Life Project; Leslie Quinn for creating space when it got crowded; Mae and Ted Frankel for the work ethic; Marilyn Anthony for getting us to tell the story; Michael Mack for affirming that a company can be way more than a business; Mordecai Finley for the path down into the soul; Paul S. Pariser for writing the check that allowed us to start construction; Poker Canyon for a place in the circle; Randi, Michele and Jennifer for all of their support, sacrifice, shifts behind the counter in the early days, patience and love; Rick Federico for time and wisdom when we needed it; Riley Lagesen for his advocacy; Ruth Dressler for the love; Sherry, Kirk and Al Oberholtzer for working opening week; Stan Bromley for giving me something to shoot for; Stephanie Chandler and the Authority Publishing team for guidance and support; Tom Jermain for the balloons; the USHG family for its hospitality.

To every person who shared in this story by being a Tender Greens guest, thank you from the bottom of our hearts. We have likely forgotten some important people on these lists. Forgive us. We apologize for any hurt feelings.

And finally, for writing books that we love gifting to others:
Howard Schultz - *Pour Your Heart Into It*
Michael Gerber - *The E-Myth*
Gary Erickson - *Raising the Bar*
Chip Conley - *Peak* and *Wisdom at Work*
Danny Meyer - *Setting the Table*
John Mackey, Rajendra Sisodia - *Conscious Capitalism*
David Allen - *Getting Things Done*
Mark Goulston - *Get Out of Your Own Way at Work*
John C. Maxwell - *The 21 Indispensable Qualities of the Leader*

CPSIA information can be obtained
at www.ICGtesting.com
Printed in the USA
FSHW010028030122
87341FS